SCHIZOPHRENIA

Robert Francis, LCSW

Schizophrenia: A Strength's Perspective

Life Lessons Learned from Living with Schizophrenia

Urano
publishing

Argentina - Chile - Colombia - Spain
USA - Mexico - Peru - Uruguay

The first edition of this book was published in January 2024

ISBN: 978-1-953027-28-3

E-ISBN: 978-1-953027-29-0

Printed in Spain

Library of Cataloging-in-Publication Data

Francis, Robert

1. Mental Health   2. Mental Awareness

Schizophrenia: A Strength's Perspective

CONTENTS

Foreword by Dr. William T. Carpenter, MD, University Maryland

Viewing schizophrenia as a doctor, responsible for clinical care, or as a research scientist, addressing specific aspects of the disorder, is quite different from knowledge based on the experience of schizophrenia. Robert Francis, the author of this book, has lived experience of schizophrenia and has also had a clinical role in helping persons with psychosis. In this book, he provides unique insights based on what he has learned from his experience with schizophrenia. He identifies 13 lessons valuable to him, which he now shares with others. He reverses the focus on adverse effects of the illness into an approach to learning from schizophrenia. This is conceptualized in an existential framework. His 13 chapters begin with existential fixations and how schizophrenia taught him how to deal with an unchosen affection.

The following chapters deal, in turn, with fixed hopelessness moving from "it is what it is" to the personal power to move from hopelessness. And how schizophrenia taught him to evaluate reality beyond the perception associated with illness. Other chapters address how to deal with deviation from cultural norms, the benefit of developing resilience, avoiding fear during psychological darkness, remediating cognitive distortions, the asset of the ability to laugh at something painful, finding your own way and accepting your own person, the ethics of kindness, vocational creativity, and how cognitive temperance can lead to reasonableness.

The issues are complex, but the message is remarkable. Lived experience with schizophrenia enabled the author to learn lessons from the experience and the challenges of illness. In this book he details what he has learned from schizophrenia and how this knowledge can enhance a person's ability to learn from schizophrenia experiences. It is a message aimed at success in coping with psychosis.

—William T. Carpenter, MD, Professor of Psychiatry, University of Maryland School of Medicine; former director of the Maryland Psychiatric Research Center; prior leader of the DSM-5 Psychosis Work Group; and Editor-in-Chief of the Schizophrenia Bulletin.

Introduction

Schizophrenia: A Strengths Perspective: Life Lessons Learned from Living with Schizophrenia is the final volume in my trilogy of books on schizophrenia. Of course, each book has its own purpose, story, and goal. *"On Conquering Schizophrenia; From the Desk of a Therapist and Survivor; With Purview on Metaphysics, Philosophy, and Theology"* was a longtime labor of love. It is philosophical, theoretical, and ultimately spiritual. *"The Essential Schizophrenia Companion; With Foreword by Elyn R. Saks, PhD, JD"* entails my mission to provide what I deem to be the absolute "essentials" for understanding schizophrenia. Such essentials include developing an insight into one's illness, learning to manage one's behavior (especially when acutely symptomatic), understanding the nature of psychosis, harnessing potential protective factors, and learning and developing one's cognitive–behavioral skills to support a stable and long-term recovery. It is my hope that once these are read, that a reader will be up to speed in comprehending schizophrenia. Both *"On Conquering Schizophrenia"* and *"The Essential Schizophrenia Companion"* carry the aims of education, ultimate recovery, and knowing that ample quality of life can be achieved despite schizophrenia.

This newest book has been an idea of mine for over a year. It has teased my intellect for some time. It is very interesting to me how a book becomes a book. Of course, it begins as an idea. But I have found that this idea must first bubble, like water in a pot on the stove. It begins as calm water until it eventually bubbles and boils. Once boiling, the idea begins to form and the pen is laid to paper. *Schizophrenia: A Strengths Perspective: Life Lessons Learned from Living with Schizophrenia* has boiled and it is due time for me to present this work.

The idea behind this book is a personal passion. The perception of schizophrenia is nearly unanimously dictated by what is referred to as the "medical deficit model". The medical deficit model entails the deficits associated with schizophrenia. These deficits are categorized according to medical "symptoms". Such symptoms include auditory hallucinations, visual hallucinations, delusions, and mood disturbances (including paranoia). Such deficits are viewed as abject hinderances to one's general well-being and as detrimental to a person's ability to function. Personally, I am no stranger to all such symptom deficits.

Auditory hallucinations are hearing voices with no logical source. Sometimes these seem to come from the environment, and other times they are from inside one's own head. While they also can be perceived as coming from another person, any such voice will lack proper interpersonal validity. They can be confounding. Visual hallucinations have been less common than auditory ones in my case, but they are visual conjurings absent requisite validity nevertheless. Over my many years, schizophrenia has induced an abundance of mood disturbances. Anxiety and depression have certainly reigned, and one might say "cavorted", but, in particular, the rascal of "paranoia" has dominated. Paranoia in schizophrenia is different than a mundane sort of suspiciousness. Paranoia, meaning the clinical paranoia associated with schizophrenia, is a fulsome and pervasive feeling of persecution from an unrelenting perceived personal vendetta and attack by others. It has the notable earmark of it being with malevolent interpersonal intent. Clinical paranoia is terrifying, but from this too I have learned to overcome.

According to the medical model, under the umbrella of each symptom are a myriad of subtypes and formations. For example, delusions can be categorized according to the clinical subtypes, known as the grandiose, persecutory, somatic, bizarre, and religious. I have experienced all such subtypes and, admittedly, they do me no favors. Delusions can also be categorized on a spectrum of agreeability based on one's observing mind (or perhaps one's ego). If a delusion is characterized as "syntonic", it follows that the delusional belief is agreeable to one's intellect or that it supports one's ego. For example, if I believed I had great wealth (but this was actually unfounded) and found such an idea to be positive and a prop, this could be labeled as syntonic; that is, agreeable and pleasing to my sensibilities. Conversely, if I assume a delusion of a "dystonic" characteristic, this would entail an idea or reference that is disagreeable to my ego and sensitivities, and it would be causative of emotional distress. If I believed the world, the entire human population, and God were out to persecute me, this would entail dystonic ideation. In no manner is this delusion pleasing—it is very disturbing. Such a disturbing belief can be labeled dystonic. All delusions can be located on the syntonic–dystonic spectrum. If the delusion leans towards "pleasing", it is said to be syntonic and if the delusion disturbs, it is said to be dystonic. This spectrum is very broad with personal experiences ranging across a broad range of capabilities.

Auditory hallucinations can also be subtyped. Two of the most prominent subtypes are known as "persecutory" and "command" auditory type hallucinations. Persecutory auditory hallucinations entail a subject hearing voices of a derogatory and persecutory nature. For example, hearing a voice that says, "Everyone hates you and we all want you dead," is a sort of persecutory auditory hallucination. In my case, at one time in the course of my illness, auditory hallucinations were grueling and gruesome. They added an additional layer to an already to dystonic psychosis. But I have learned and overcome them since then. Nevertheless, persecutory auditory hallucinations can be distressing. The second subtype of auditory hallucinations is known as command auditory hallucinations. Such voices will direct (or command) the subject to undertake a certain type of action or actions. For example, the voice may command, "I want you to kill yourself." I mention this specific example to highlight the important need for those with schizophrenia, and their families, to understand the underlying potential peril of command auditory hallucinations. Personally, I have experienced this sort of danger. Very early in the course of my illness, command auditory hallucinations were extremely dangerous to my survival. I was fortunate to endure them, especially when these were an unknown entity to me. Command auditory hallucinations can cause someone with schizophrenia to commit suicide, particularly when an individual is unfamiliar with the phenomenon. As a therapist, when working with those with schizophrenia, I am always very upfront about telling my clients to never follow the commands of any auditory hallucinations. They can be perilous. Finally, visual hallucinations are not clinically parsed according to subtypes but they can surely be evaluated on the syntonic–dystonic spectrum.

When someone is actively psychotic, that is, divorced from reality due to a combination of symptoms, one's ability to function can be significantly impaired. Schizophrenia, in clinical speak, is oftentimes referred to as an "SPMI", this being the abbreviation of "severe and persistent mental illness." Given the dual characteristics of severity and persistence (or chronicity), it can be understood that schizophrenia comes with challenges. Sometimes, those with schizophrenia have better times than others. Sometimes, symptoms diminish or abate somewhat. The illness of schizophrenia is not homogeneous, it is heterogeneous. Homogeneous indicates uniformity whereas heterogeneous indicates variability. The complete symptom profile of each person will be variable. Nevertheless, for those with schizophrenia, common themes and common symptoms occur. Exactly as described? No. Similar? Yes. Based on the severity and persistence of one's illness, it will often follow an according prognosis with specific recovery outcomes. For example, sometimes, working may be well tolerated, but at other times it is simply not viable. Interpersonal behavior may be easier sometimes compared to other times. Routine daily functioning, for example, activities such as good hygiene, chore engagement, and participation in daily personal responsibilities, may wax and wane based on the acute symptom profile status. I will have you know, however, that I passionately believe in and espouse recovery. Recovery entails a sense of stability, both for the individual and their family (if indeed family applies). Recovery is the wider aim; it entails a temporal sort of homeostasis. Homeostasis is the phenomenon of a system's ability to regulate and stabilize itself over time. When a temporal sort of stability is achieved by an individual and their family, recovery is actuated. Acuity may flare, but, according to the wider scope, the system remains stable and the individual and family remain in a comfortable system balance. Recovery is a temporal perspective and it undermines the persistence to schizophrenia. Severity indeed may be triggered by the formation of acute symptoms, but one can learn to manage such flares ups in favor of an extended temporal stability. Recovery equates to a comfortable system stability over time. The work to be done here is the achievement of this stability and therein lies my mission to help.

The medical model is the overwhelming primary view of schizophrenia. Please do not misconstrue my intentions here, I have no qualms with the medical model. In fact, I deem it accurate. I mean that. Although the "deficit" model is equated to the medical model, it does not mean a lack of personal individual strengths—not in the least. The medical model, as a "deficit" model, equates clinical framework and conceptualization, but it is certainly not any sort of personality dig. It is a model that addresses inherent problems. It is not a value judgment of "lacking" character. So please do not assume that I reject the medical model, because certainly I do not. I embrace it. It saved my life.

Schizophrenia entails a unique and different type of perspective. It is simply a new and different perspective, and complimentary one at that. I have lived with schizophrenia for more than 25 years now. I have taken antipsychotic medication each and every day for these 25 years. In this sense, the medical model has buoyed my recovery. I fear what that the results may have been without my medications.

In this book, however, I am driven by a unique perspective. It is a perspective that glimpses the personal strength gleaned from living with schizophrenia. I consider schizophrenia both a friend and a foe. It has instilled in me both terror and triumph. In my early 20s, with the initial onset of my schizophrenia, the symptoms were an absolute terror. It is important to know that, at the time, I had no reference points regarding schizophrenia. I knew nothing of its characteristics from my generalized education, nor was it present in my family and lineage. I was ignorant of it. Given this, with its initial onset, its inducements intensely frightened me and I had no insight. I was experiencing a terribly disturbing psychosis, and I did not know that it was psychosis, which further lent to my psychosis two-fold. Ignorance and schizophrenia are not bliss. Now, when I think back on that time, I count my lucky stars that I survived. It was a time of great peril for me. Because of the disturbing psychosis, I often thought about suicide. At the time, I was experiencing persecutory perceptions. I believed that everyone was fervently against me. I felt entirely persecuted and alone. I thought I was hated by all others and it was terrifying and persistent. I was significantly delusional but, at the time, I perceived it to be my accurate and unrelenting reality. Oftentimes, the initial onset phase can be similarly perilous for many with schizophrenia, in particular due to its novelty and a lack of understanding and recognition. I consider it a personal triumph that I persisted amid my fright and survived the onslaught. It was the darkest of times, but I escaped physically unscathed. A triumph of great proportions.

In my experience with schizophrenia, I have experienced the full spectrum, from defeat to redemption. In terms of psychological defeat, I have at times felt a deep sense of hopelessness and despair. When your reality appears thoroughly doomed, it is difficult to remain optimistic and hopeful. A lack of hope can be a primary variable supportive of depression and I navigated these psychological waters. I have learned, however, from this sense of hopelessness. I have learned that hope is indeed a variable and, further, it can be cultivated and coddled. In returning from a sense of hopelessness to optimism and an irrefutable sense of persistent hopefulness, I found redemption. Schizophrenia, at once, instructed me on psychological defeat but failed in its persuasion. Rather, I gleaned a potent intangible lesson on the personal characteristics of unrelenting hope. This reigns as the key to my redemption.

Schizophrenia has instructed me regarding dark times versus brighter times. Schizophrenia has taught me about the value of suffering and it has provided me lessons on the spectrum of psychological dark versus psychological light. I have learned from schizophrenia that life often casts shadows, and further, I have learned that this is universal to us all, not only to those with schizophrenia. At times, we all tread amid psychological dread. Schizophrenia taught me about bleakness. But, more importantly, it taught me not to fear dark times as it is simply parcel to being a human. Schizophrenia has also, conversely, instructed me on how to be grateful and appreciative of life's lighter moments. I have only come to appreciate the lighter times of life relative to my travails amongst shadows. Schizophrenia taught me the universality of suffering, but, at the same time, it instructed me regarding appreciation and gratefulness when things are copacetic. No longer do I fear dark times, or abjectly try to avoid them, for this is forlorn. Schizophrenia has taught me about the full psychological spectrum of the dark versus the light. According to this lesson, I have learned about the inimitable texture of life and this now exists as a boon.

Schizophrenia, a once treacherous and unwanted foe, ultimately has forged intangible positive personal qualities. It has instigated positive perspectives, both of self and of the world around me. Schizophrenia has taught me a great deal regarding myself, others, and about life in general. I am now inspired—my idea at a full boil—to share with you, my cherished reader, such life lessons. Each chapter presents a lesson. And each lesson was derived from my experiences with schizophrenia.

I feel I have been exposed to too much of a generalized doom and gloom regarding schizophrenia. Certainly, and by vast majority, media representations are unfavorable. A certain sort of generalized societal stigma too often prevails. Those living with schizophrenia are often portrayed as dangerous, unstable, and the prototype of "crazy". Those living with schizophrenia are often publicly perceived as incapable of living productive lives and are incapable of significant contributions. I am compelled to push back on such misguided notions. I do not believe I have ever seen, read, heard, felt, or sensed a celebration of schizophrenia. As such, *Schizophrenia: A Strengths Perspective: Life Lessons Learned from Living with Schizophrenia* is a celebration of sorts. It is about healthy coping perspectives, gleaned from schizophrenia, and applied to our shared normative knowledge, life itself.

Chapter 1

Existential Fixations

Life lesson—Life is often imposed, not chosen.

When I was in my early 20s, I was diagnosed with "schizophrenia, paranoid type". The diagnosis came after months of erratic behavior, erratic speech, and delusional occupancy. Because my psychosis was initially gradual and incremental, a severe mental illness was not initially obvious, especially to me and my family. But in the end, my psychosis became florid and obvious. My family supported me as I was introduced to the mental health treatment system; I am most fortunate I had their support. Adverse outcomes often result during the first onset of psychosis due to its element of surprise. When schizophrenia first appears, most commonly in early adulthood, often, the affected individual and the surrounding social support (i.e., family) cannot clearly understand the cause of the subtle, but ultimately profound, personality change. During this initial onset time, very poor outcomes often ensue due to unfamiliarity with schizophrenia.

Many times, during this first onset, due to a malevolent psychosis, individuals may face any number of poor outcomes, including criminality, harm-to-self or others, damage to the family and/or alienation from primary social supports, homelessness, job loss and/or unemployment, along with other potential high-risk behaviors with potential punitive outcomes. This is why jails are often filled with those experiencing mental illness. Young adults with first-onset psychosis may behave in manners that are entirely different from their otherwise tempered dispositions and personalities. It can be tragic. I was fortunate to escape this time of peril unscathed. I know many others with schizophrenia who have not been as fortunate as me—as such, my sympathies run deep.

Life is often imposed, and not chosen. I call life impositions "existential fixations". Certain elements of life, simply and undeniably, are imposed; this applies to you, me, and everyone else. For me, life imposed schizophrenia and, for the duration of my life, ontology. I certainly had no choice in this acquisition. Life presented me with schizophrenia; unchosen, unwanted, and rather indifferently.

It took me many years to understand life's impositions as "existential fixations". What I eventually learned was that existential fixations are universal and not simply specific to me. Each and every human will be faced with their own existential fixations. For some, it may be schizophrenia, but it exists alongside unquantifiable other variables. Existential fixations seem to me nearly infinite in how they present. For greater context, I offer the following existential fixations as examples. Such impositions to each may include disease (in all its myriad presentations), family of origin characteristics, location of birth, gender, tragic accidents, financial hardship, famine, and natural disasters. No single existential fixation is chosen. No one chooses disease or famine. It is imposed. So how does awareness of existential fixations improve one's ability to cope across a lifespan?

I have come to deeply understand that it is not simply schizophrenia that is imposed. I did not choose schizophrenia, nor opt in its favor. It was laid at my doorstep and I had to open the door. I have come to realize, however, that schizophrenia is simply a singular imposition among a more general universal cache. I have come to understand schizophrenia as a possible existential fixation among many. Schizophrenia is my imposition. But, assuredly, you too have yours, be it schizophrenia or another of the vast options.

How has the recognition of existential fixations improved my life? Firstly, it has taught me the power of acceptance. Long ago, I came to terms with the acceptance of my schizophrenia. Prior to acceptance, I was mired in a "Why me?" form of personal pity. No longer, however. In fact, schizophrenia, as my primary existential fixation, I now view as a lighted imposition, compared to the possible myriad of sufferings possible. I have come to terms with my imposed and unchosen schizophrenia. I know I can manage it, that is, in a general sense. Surely, acuities may occur and cause distress, but, in general, I know I can successfully live with them and cope with them. When I look to those around me and compare my challenges with schizophrenia to the imposed challenges of others, I often consider myself fortunate to have avoided a greater source of suffering, which I surely recognize at times in others. I now know that others suffer well beyond my own experiences, and I now view my schizophrenia as a comparably light sort of imposition. With the recognition of a universal state of suffering, which is among us all, it lends to the acceptance of whatever imposed conditions may be. Only by first accepting can capable coping follow. Absorbing and appreciating the existential fixations applied to us all can certainly deepen our empathy for one another. Suffering abounds, and it is important to understand both the source and etiology, that is, oftentimes an affliction imposed lends greater clarity in life. It is unanimous. We all suffer. The only distinction is its form. No one is alone in suffering.

I now see schizophrenia as a lighted form of suffering. If you live just one day with an acute awareness of existential fixations, the common human affliction of suffering can be revealed. Once aware that suffering is a global and universal experience, it becomes most difficult to engage with the question of "Why me?". I have accepted my lot. My empathy has deepened, like a vast deep ocean, when I meet another's form of suffering with recognition. I see you suffer, too. Further, I see your affliction, too, just as unchosen. The only matter becomes the distinction of each's type and form of suffering. The question is not *if* we will suffer. We all suffer. Oftentimes, malaise will be rendered to each, and all, without singular choice. This recognition of existential fixations has opened my eyes to the suffering beyond my ego-centered self. I see the reality of human nature. We all suffer, regardless of status or position. In this sense, human nature is communal. I cross the interpersonal bridge by manner of understanding, through empathy for your troubles and your travails, rather than a persistent personal preoccupation (and perhaps self-pity). Schizophrenia has taught me about unchosen afflictions. It has taught me about suffering, as much a part of you as of me. So, I rejoice in our commonality and I abandon self-centered notions of suffering. I have come to celebrate our mutualities, especially when times are good, and I have dismissed any sense of personal pity. This recognition of common suffering has opened my eyes to human nature. And I have schizophrenia to thank for this.

Chapter 2

Life as Quantum

Lesson—Life is quantum, not determined.

The character of schizophrenia has caused me to often contemplate the nature and fabric of reality. After all, schizophrenia entails psychosis, when active that is. And what is psychosis? Simply stated, psychosis entails an individual breached from "reality". Which therefore begs the question, if I am breached from reality, what is reality proper?

Metaphysics is the branch of science that deals with the nature of reality. In a general manner, over the course of human history and its associated scientific exploration, two metaphysical explanations regarding the fabric of reality have been proposed. This metaphysical duo involves scientific "determinism" versus a scientific "quantum" perspective. Scientific determinism has dominated for centuries, but is now antiquated given recent quantum sciChapter 2entific discoveries. Of course, the concept of reality is immensely important in the context of the illness of schizophrenia. Reality is a primary defining characteristic associated with psychosis and schizophrenia, and is therefore of utmost relevance. From my own curiosity, when I learned and understood that my psychosis was a breach from reality, I pondered what so-called "reality" was. If I needed to remain under the constraints of reality, I thought that understanding its entity was essential. I therefore investigated the study of reality, metaphysics, further.

According to theory, metaphysical determinism entails a sort of exactness, while the quantum perspective entails a sort of possibility. For example, determinism is qualified by mathematical certitude. Derivative scientific theories of the world, driven by determinism, will reside on a bedrock of exact equations. For example, $2 + 2 = 4$, is a type of determined equation. You may agree, this proposition is most difficult to dispute. From about the 1950s onward, however, with advances in technology, humans began observing the world with new capabilities and lenses. With new metaphysical evidence, the understanding of reality shifted from terse equations, deterministic types of equations, to possibilities and probabilities rather than any type of determined necessity. This shift, away from determinism to a world of probabilities and possibilities, has transformed our modern conception of metaphysics, i.e., of the nature of reality (matter and time included).

What does all this have to do with schizophrenia? When schizophrenia had me by the neck, I strongly believed that reality was determined. I believed that reality was a strict sort of necessary equation. I believed reality to be $2 + 2 = 4$. I believed, akin to the vernacular, "it is what it is". This belief of mine held me captive for a long time in what I believed was an unalterable reality. I believed my psychosis, my then-experience of the world, was just as fixed as $2 + 2 = 4$. Therefore, I saw no escape from my psychosis. Such a belief was not only dooming, terrifying, and tormenting, it was nearly absent of any sense for change. I am fortunate that I survived this long period of hopelessness. During that time, my mental status was tortured. I believed that the universe, all its inhabitants (God included), were directly out to get to me. I felt entirely persecuted, alone, isolated, forsaken, and forlorn. I nearly believed that I was out of options and that my torment was an unalterable existential predicament. I only survived this time because of a sliver of hope; this hope being that, by some miracle, serendipity, or radical turn of events, this malevolent experience would somehow terminate. During that time, I was barely hanging on. My life could not have been more miserable. My survival persisted because of the faintest hope. I will have you know that hope is an amazing intangible thing. Oftentimes, it is our sole form of preservation. Without hope, we are doomed. With hope, we are preserved and perhaps inspired. Hope now resides in my means of coping as an exquisite tool. Hope is now essential in my life. I keep regular tabs on my degree of hopefulness and when it is faint or substantially lacking, I double (or perhaps triple) my efforts. As a therapist, when it is pertinent, I will talk to my clients about hope. Hope can work miracles. I've seen it, both in myself and others.

Once I changed my inherent belief, from one of a necessary determinism to an updated and corrected form of quantum soup, I found my cognitive recourse. A quantum worldview changed my psychology and ultimately my life. Once I came to understand that I had the capacity to influence my metaphysical gestalt, I acquired a recourse in my pushbacks against psychosis. I no longer thought my psychosis was necessarily fixed or unalterable. I now grasped, very viscerally, that I could have cognitive influence over my experience of the world, psychosis included. I embraced the quantum principles of probabilities, possibilities, and likelihoods rather than a life that was necessarily qualified or already determined. I gained a sense of personal influence regarding my oft-terrifying psychosis. No longer was psychosis fixed. No longer did I believe that, "it is what it is". I was empowered to change my psychosis into a more rational type of psychological grounding. I now had the psychological belief and tools to parlay my own psychology into a much more stable and temperate ontology. I was no longer powerless over my psychosis. I was empowered to chase away my psychosis. Life and psychosis were no longer determined. It was a quantum soup of possibility and potential. Schizophrenia taught me about my own influence over my experience of the world. With this recognition, things like determination, effort, self-control, and personal responsibility flooded the grounds. Schizophrenia taught me that "it is what it is" is not necessarily so. We have the capacity for choice.

Schizophrenia taught me the power of attitude. Life is not dictatorial. We can influence our lives according to our attitudes and chosen behaviors. In my case, I use my chosen attitude to dissuade any psychotic influences. Additionally, accordingly, I choose healthy behaviors that also diminish the residue of cognitive psychosis. For example, maintaining good sleep routines, managing my stress, eating well, exercising, and ample engagement in my daily responsibilities all support diminishing the traces of a detrimental psychosis, be it subtle or acute. I learned that, in many ways, that my ultimate fate and outcome (schizophrenia relevant or not) comes from my attitude and my behaviors—and supremely so. Oftentimes, aside from imposed existential fixations, our chosen attitudes and behaviors certainly matter and make a terrific difference. Once this is acknowledged, however, the awesome responsibility of our existential choosings follows. We must embrace choice and we must assume utmost responsibility. Responsibility becomes the foe and adversary to existential fixations. Responsibility is the antidote to such impositions. Once I learned that I had a responsibility to manage my psychosis, i.e., my perceptions of myself and the world around me, my life changed and I assumed those responsibilities. I assumed responsibility for managing my schizophrenia. Ultimately, schizophrenia instructed me regarding my capacity for choices. This lesson provided a further foundation for my recovery and to further gainful living.

Chapter 3

Perception is Not (Necessarily) Reality

Lesson—Perception is not always reality.

Philosopher David Hume, circa 1700, posited "esse est percipi". According to its translation, we arrive at "perception is reality". Hume's seminal posit, perception is reality, has since capably seeped into our modern vernacular so much that it capably resides as a tried and true idiom. But in so much as it's now common, is "perception is reality" a necessary truism?

Diving straight to the point, if you live with schizophrenia, this common idiom carries great pertinence. Firstly, allow me a brief elucidation on why perception applies so prominently to the schizophrenia syndrome. Schizophrenia is a neuropsychiatric condition that substantially infiltrates our perception of the world around us. The "psychosis" of schizophrenia is primarily derived as secondary to our "perceptions" of the world. Psychosis is sensory. It abides by an integrative sensory experience of the world. For example, in both you and me, our senses, together, create an overall picture of the world. When one looks at a tree, a sophisticated neurobiological process provides us with a mental picture of the tree. When one sees the tree, the brain is coordinating our visual sensibilities and is translating meaning to our consciousness of the concept of a "tree". This underlying neurobiological mechanism is automatic, and functions without need for effort or intention. The outcome of this process is known as "perception". Perception is the sum total of one's sensory inputs and their translation, according to an identified sort of meaning based on one's awareness. For most, I believe, perception is taken for granted without fervent and undue need for substantial questioning. But, if one lives with schizophrenia, it is understood that perception is its own inherent sort of malaise.

For those living with schizophrenia, what is known as perception can be significantly misguided, that is, in comparison to the psychological norm. For example, in revisiting our tree example, you and I see the same tree. When you see the tree, you see one of nature's aesthetics. When I see the tree, as someone living with schizophrenia with an active psychosis, I hear it's rustling leaves as a hideous sort of voice, espousing malevolent content. It's certainly the same tree, but my sensory integration and the associated meanings are significantly misguided from the norm.

The idiom "if it looks like a duck, quacks like a duck, it's a duck" nicely aligns by analogy to "perception is reality". This duck idiom, for most, may be a certain truism and therefore naturally and easily accepted. Similar to my tree analogy, when you see the duck you see another one of nature's aesthetic creations. You see a duck according to its nature, feathers, bill, etc. When I see the duck, and I am amid an active psychosis, I potentially see an active actor involved with others in some sort of a sinister and malevolent plot. It is the same inherent creature but our perceptions are much different. In regards to schizophrenia, this I label a neurological snafu. Therefore, I have learned, via living with schizophrenia, that "perception" does not equate universally to reality, and further yet, that reality can be interpreted well beyond simple sensory perception.

I have learned not to overly rely solely on my sensory perceptions. The schizophrenia active render, that being the "psychosis", relies heavily on my perceptions of the world. The things I perceive, see, and hear contribute to the grounding of the psychosis. Psychosis becomes embedded in my sensory experience of the world. Human beings, when fortunate, have five primary functioning senses, and it is through these senses that they experience the world. The combination of one's sensory input and its integration combine to create our perception of the world. Perception is the result of the sum total of our sensory inputs. Our perception, then, becomes our view of the world. It is how the world appears or seems (to us). For example, consider the phenomenon of dizziness. When one becomes dizzy due to a sensory change or manipulation, the perception of the world, while dizzy, looks different from normal. Consider schizophrenia and its associated perceptions akin to a state of acute dizziness. With an active psychosis, the world looks and feels different from the norm. In this way, schizophrenia lurks and dwells amid the senses that produce a perception of the world. This perception, at times, is skewed and at times by varying severities. My psychosis is so real because it is immediately "perceived". But, if we retreat into the definition of psychosis, that being, a detachment from so-called reality, I note that a sort of dualism, or perhaps a paradox, is readily assumed amid my perceptions.

From living with schizophrenia, I have learned about what I deem its inherent dualism or its paradox. For example, and returning to the duck analogy, upon me looking at the duck, because of my psychosis, and now my learnedness regarding its often-faulty perceptions, I no longer fully trust my perception; in this case, of the duck. Yes, I see a duck. But I certainly do not trust the perception as being entirely accurate or truthful. Rather, I have come to feel a sort of ease with my perceptions. Whether or not it is indeed a duck or not is not my primary concern. Rather, my primary concern entails me maintaining my rational behavior in response to the duck. I no longer entirely care regarding the content of my perceptions, i.e., the duck. Maintaining a decorum to my behavior, whatever the given perception, is now my top priority. My perceptions can, at times, be marked by ideations of persecution, for example, but I now consequently take my perceptions with an easiness and a lack of any great intensity. I do not want to unnecessarily flood my feelings with a sense of persecution. My perceptions serve as a sort of veneer to my world, and I do not place utmost confidence in any such appearances. I certainly see a duck, but, cognitively, I say to myself, "ok, perhaps a duck." Although I plainly see the duck, because of living with schizophrenia, such a perception carries no veracity. This is the dualism and paradox of perceptions with schizophrenia.

Living with schizophrenia has taught me about faulty perceptions. Be they the combination of a neurological snafu and extreme cognitive distortions, perceptions with schizophrenia become highly skewed from normative reality. Symptoms of schizophrenia can follow, derived from skewed perceptions, including delusions. Delusions are false beliefs. These are beliefs without a requisite evidence for truth. When the world presents as skewed, or otherwise stated, when I am amid an acute psychosis, certain beliefs may ensue from my perceptions. Being that my perceptions are inherently skewed, it logically follows that derivative beliefs from skewed perceptions can result in delusions. Delusions are an extreme sort of cognitive distortion. For example, at one time I believed I was communicating with people on TV while I was watching from my living room. This is a delusion because it lacks the requisite evidence in support. Such delusions are characterized by a robust cognitive distortion. We all experience cognitive distortions, schizophrenia or otherwise. The difference with schizophrenia, however, is that such cases are profoundly distorted (rather than minimally). There are many subtypes of cognitive distortions. Cognitive behavioral therapy has done an excellent job in identifying and elucidating cognitive distortions. Such cognitive distortions include, for example, terms known as all-or-nothing thinking, catastrophizing, overgeneralizing, selective abstraction, jumping to conclusions, and black-and-white thinking. Cognitive distortions are a sort of irrationality. Delusions are a sort of hyper-irrationality.

I tell you, though, psychotic perceptions present to my sensory faculties as highly real and certainly persuasive. If psychosis were not persuasive it would not substantiate. Given that schizophrenia

skews the intellect, producing perceptions well external to normative reality, an alternative sort of solution-focused recourse must
follow.

Returning to my duck analogy, that being, "if it looks like a
duck and quacks like a duck, it's a duck", allow me to elucidate
on a type of knowing that is external to the sole faculties of perception. If needed, reality can be construed beyond mere perception. There is more than one way to "skin a cat," so to speak.
External to perception, reality can be construed otherwise. For
example, the duck can be internally visualized, and thought about
by manner of an internal dialogue. The duck concept can be amplified or deconstructed. The duck can be compared to similar
animals to be better understood. In the self-construction of reality, means avail beyond mere perception. For example, and in my
case, rather than solely relying on perception, I often construct
my experience of the world based on my personal values. I assume and project such personal values as goodness, decency, kindness, and altruism. Living my life from this center provides me a
life texture similar to perception, but of another conduit. Additionally, I often construct my reality by managing my own behavior and I try to do so at all times in the most reasonable manner
and accord, including behaviors that will be viewed as reasonable
given a specific social context. I also will tap into the intangible of
hopefulness as I cavort across my day and this, in of itself, coalesces into a type of experienced personal reality. Generally speaking,
I use these types of self-inducements to overcome my faulty perceptions. Perception alone no longer has me by the tail.

In the end, schizophrenia has taught me to evaluate my reality beyond mere perception. Reality is malleable. It can be

constructed rather than being passively absorbed. There's so much more to life beyond the veneer of appearance. I assure you, at times, perception can dupe itself. In the end, to conclude my duck analogy: it looked like a duck, it quacked like a duck, but ultimately it turned out to be a fox hunter's stuffed faux bait and lure. Schizophrenia taught me to think a little deeper. To analyze a little deeper. In regards to the reality construct, schizophrenia taught me to temporally and procedurally self-construct my vision of reality rather relying solely on my perceptions. And, in the end, the duck may just may be a stuffed imitation and lure.

Chapter 4

"The Best Laid Plans…"

Lesson—Life does not always follow a script

Sometimes, life politely follows the script. When it does so, I call this the "charmed life". For some, life oftentimes follows according to a very natural developmental progression. For example, perhaps, a charmed life script may entail a progression such as: a good childhood, educational attainment, romantic relationship, gainful employment, career pursuits, marriage, house, and family. It reads like the American dream. I find this to be charming. Please do not misunderstand me, however, I harbor no ill will to those who live a charmed existence. Quite the contrary, I actually root for such outcomes. For why would I harbor such an ill intent for others? But, I must add, that I find the charmed life a fascinating observation. I assure you, beyond the charming, there is much, much more to the global life story, for each and every one of us.

Personally, my own life was charming for a good long while and I certainly recognize this good fortune. I was raised by a great family and had a great upbringing. My childhood, in fact, was nothing short of magical, and a very happy sort of magic at that. But, fast forwarding to around my early 20s, that was when my "best laid plans" began to fall apart.

The short version is that in my early 20s, after finishing college and while working in my then-chosen field of broadcasting, a gradual and incremental psychosis infiltrated my once rational cognitive functioning. Why schizophrenia entered my life remains unknown, but it certainly influenced my life's script and its course. Schizophrenia has long since been scientifically studied. Unfortunately, at this time, its exact etiology continues to baffle and confuse. We do not know with any assuredness as to why schizophrenia initiates. Certainly, conjectures abound. For example, some hypotheses include a genetic combination, or, otherwise, perhaps organic brain deficits. Some posit diathesis. Diathesis is when an underlying latent biological condition becomes active given a requisite amount of applied personal stress. In other words, stress induces the appearance of the disease. We do not know why schizophrenia occurs. Its etiology certainly remains a subject of prolific scientific study. Once its etiology is confirmed, I am sure that the best treatments will then follow. In my case, it took some eight months, I would estimate, before a florid psychosis took hold.

Initially, my experiences with psychosis were subtle. Its full activation took time. But, with each passing day, my auditory hallucinations increased along with associative delusions. Ultimately, due to an increasing psychosis, my behavior, speech, and interpersonal characteristic became increasingly erratic. After my mental illness was no longer hidden from others, I was then formally and appropriately introduced into the mental health system. So much for my charmed script.

From around age 22 to 24, my life was primarily about trying to recover from schizophrenia and establish some stability in my life. After my second psychiatric hospitalization, I attended Continuing Day Treatment (CDT, a now defunct modality). Continuing Day Treatment was an outpatient mental health program that spanned the day. Generally speaking, I attended CDT from 9 am to 2 pm daily. I did this Monday through Friday for some nine months.

When attending CDT, I took personal stock of my life status. Clearly my "best laid plans" were quite defunct. I do not think my life script included learning to live with schizophrenia while attending an adult mental health program. Certainly, my charmed life was off its rails. At the time, it was disconcerting to say the least. But once again, schizophrenia taught me a valuable life lesson, that being, life "plans" often get disrupted and such disruptions do not only occur in others.

I think I was dismayed by my life circumstances, in part, because I was comparing my generalized prevailing lot and circumstances to a vast multitude of "others", including my peers, family members, and, more generally, to an assumed sort of life norm. When I evaluated my circumstances, most of my external comparisons were ostensibly unfavorable. I was not so much "getting ahead" in life as I was treading water and surviving. Along with learning about how life plans can go to askew, I concurrently learned the lesson of trying not to compare myself with others.

Schizophrenia taught me that a normal life progression is more myth than fact. Oftentimes, one's life plans can quickly divert. This can happen in life, at any time, across the full lifespan, and in a myriad of ways and predicaments. For example, emergent disease can quickly disrupt one's life. The types of different diseases are seemingly innumerable. Motor vehicle accidents can quickly change lives. Natural disasters can hurt people and properties. War and famine may occur. Victimization by violent crime happens and can have lasting consequences. Personally, I had a close family member who was burned over his entire body. In mere moments his life was changed forever. Certainly, lives can abruptly change and our plans can be quickly upended. I learned that such circumstances occur for many, myself included.

Schizophrenia taught me that obstacles present themselves in life to one and all, and that it is just a matter of time before a life monkey wrench intervenes and disrupts. No one crosses the great life divide without their own lot of disruption and associated acrimony. It is just a matter of "when", not "if". Schizophrenia taught me early on that the "best laid plans" would be faced with disruption and that it was an inevitable occurrence. Eventually, we all must improvise, and this is universal.

When certain circumstances coalesce to interfere with our chosen plans and goals, be they due to specific health factors or any number of other possible detrimental inevitabilities, we must be willing to charter a new course. Our goals may remain, but the most direct route to them might be complicated. A circuitous route may be required, or even, perhaps, an alteration of personal goals may be best or necessary. In response to our potentially obscured life plans, secondary to life's unexpected obstacles, sometimes, a certain sort of creativity may be required as we push forward. During these times, when our best laid plans are for the moment obscured, having an open mind regarding other life possibilities will help. In fact, when our goals and plans are rendered defunct, new opportunities may emerge. In response to such obstacles, such life improvisation may entail recognizing new life opportunities and/or acknowledging a new path or means to achieve our goals. Sometimes the most direct path to our goals is not a straight line, but rather is characterized as a roundabout. When our plans are tossed into the air, amid unexpected life quandaries and obstacles, reassessing and reformulating our needs and goals belies a sort of life improvisation. Such an improvisation also entails an essential sort of life creativity, that is, redefining a requisite chartered course for the future. When our best laid plans are obscured, tapping into creativity, including an acute reevaluation of life, is an important skill and can lead us forward along a new chartered course. Have no fear in such improvisation.

Schizophrenia taught me that life does not always adhere to societal norms. Actually, disruption to one's life is the norm. Only some come to understand this sooner rather than later (including many in childhood). The corollary to all this is how we react to life's disruptions. Indeed, life will be interrupted, but can we redefine, reassess, react, overcome, and transcend? This follows as the challenge. Schizophrenia has taught me that life inevitably gets disrupted, and I am thankful for yet another inherent life lesson.

Chapter 5

On Resilience

Lesson—Bouncing back is a skill.

At times, schizophrenia hurts, often substantially. Nothing across my emotional lifespan has induced more psychological pain and torment than my issues with an active psychosis. Psychosis certainly rains on the picnic.

Psychosis packs a psychological punch like no other. It can induce a singular type of psychological dismay. Psychosis can linger in my psychology and trigger significant turbulence. At worst, schizophrenia's malaise can cause one to approach hopelessness. If I buy into the persuasion of psychosis, it will certainly arrive arm in arm with a sense of hopelessness. Why associated hopelessness?

External to schizophrenia, many people experience depression and, oftentimes, hopelessness accompanies it. There may be a subtle distinction, however, between the reasons for depression in schizophrenia versus a depression absent of psychosis, or rather, the more commonly known sort of depression that many experience at one time or another. In common depression, its constituents may certainly show variability. Sometimes depression can be triggered by external events or circumstances. When depression is triggered externally, it is known as exogenous depression. Such externals may involve, for example, the loss of a job and income, death of a someone close, or grappling with the onset of a disease. These exist as possible external triggers to depression. Endogenous depression is another sort of depression. Endogenous depression is known as an existing depression, void of any necessary external trigger. For example, one's external life factors may be wholly satisfactory. One's job, family, and health may all be adequate, and perhaps even wonderful. Nevertheless, despite such given agreeability, someone may still experience depression with no known specific external source. This is the nature of endogenous depression—it is internally derived. Contrary to exogenous and endogenous types of depression, however, depression in schizophrenia may exist with a subtle distinction. Depression in schizophrenia is oftentimes derived because of a sort of perceived and inextricable macro existential entanglement. Such an entanglement, in schizophrenia, may render through the perception of reality. In schizophrenia, when one believes an entirely malevolent existence is unavoidable and will persist across one's life without possibility of abatement, existential doom may be experienced. The depression is triggered by psychotic perceptions. Without any perceived hope for change, significant depression may follow, potentially including issues of suicidality in all its nuance. In routine depression, oftentimes, someone can perceive capacity for change. In schizophrenia, however, depression may be experienced because of the absence of any perceived capacity for change. Herein can be found a subtle distinction. Psychosis can present as a "fixed" reality, absent of any type of perceived recourse. When feeling no recourse, hope can evaporate like the morning dew. Without hope, depression is inevitable.

I have learned to cultivate hope. I refuse to believe in the ever-persuasive "fixed" status of psychosis, although it often presents with that veneer. But with a sense of hope, psychosis has no teeth and retreats to its respective periphery. Hope substantially aids in repelling it.

Make no mistake, resilience is a skill. It is an essential skill in managing schizophrenia. I certainly continue to refine its sterling value. Resilience is the art of bouncing back. Now and again, psychosis comes with very dark times, but resilience can significantly undermine its treacherous power.

Psychological darkness plus psychological darkness, for me, no longer equates to psychological darkness. In stacking darkness on darkness, I have discovered fire. When schizophrenia induces gloom, whether it be persecuted feelings, rigorous anxiety, or feelings of forlorn social isolation, such an imposition will no longer steamroll my enthusiasm. Rather, I have learned to cultivate a deliberate internal hope.

Hope cultivates so much, resilience included. Amid a wholesome hope, the many layers and stacks to my perceived problems and tricky predicaments can vanish, and sometimes at once and sometimes altogether. Given ample hope, the gloom of schizophrenia can diminish, withdraw, and ultimately vanish. When ample hope abides in my disposition, I view it as a quantifiable tipping point. Once hope is capably cultivated, the psychological moroseness passes and is replaced with a bounty of ease, optimism, and renewed perspective. Hope looks to me like a light being turned on in a dark room. The surroundings may be the same, but I can now see my path forward. The weight of the world lifts and a dispositional ease and peace ensues. When such moroseness falls in favor of a lighted hope, there's no life aesthetic quite like it.

Resilience is the art of bouncing back. Further, it is the art of bouncing back as quickly as possible, without unnecessary psychological lingering. Psychosis, indeed, induces dark times. In my experience, the darkest of my ontology and of my life. But no longer does psychological distress abide by hopelessness. I refuse to view psychosis as "fixed". Consequently, hope becomes the nemesis of my schizophrenia like no other. Hope becomes a lighted psychological source and casts its power over psychotic vulnerability. Once a sense of hopefulness can be cultivated, learned, and applied, the essential skill of resilience comes to the playground.

If you live with schizophrenia, psychological tests and challenges are a given, without question. However, I have learned not to shelter in its obnoxious render. I have learned to hike into the light. I have learned that dark times will be customary; but, I have learned not to dwell in the casting of shadows. I have accepted that, at times, schizophrenia proffers a psychological gloom. But, built on the back of hopefulness, I have learned to steadfastly avoid unnecessarily lingering in any such psychological shadows. I want the lighted and I intend to move in that direction.

Certainly, healthy behaviors can follow from healthy attitudes. For me, however, moving towards the light is specified primarily as an attitude rather than any specific behavior (or behaviors). From schizophrenia, I have learned that, at times, life will cast shadows and may lead to one, at times, becoming a sort of despair or doom. Also from schizophrenia, however, I have learned that a positive attitude can significantly assuage such a feeling of doom, and strongly so. Moving from doom to another state, that being a cognitive light or perhaps a simple cognitive neutrality, entails the action mechanism of resilience. Contrary to states of depression and disturbance, my cognitive light entails an enthusiastic sense of hope with associated optimism, confidence, and even dabs of serenity when all is well-aligned. Such a mechanism of movement across the full emotional spectrum rests heavily on the variable of resilience. Moving away from the dark into a light is the art of resilience.

Resilience universally applies to us all. No one lives life without their own adversities, schizophrenia or otherwise. Learning to maneuver away from one's troubles back to the clarified light, that is, a return to agreeable mood, is the art of resilience. Further, learning to bounce back as quickly as possible is yet another additional skill. Schizophrenia has taught me resilience. I thank schizophrenia again for the life lesson.

Chapter 6

Mind Your Own Business

Lesson—Minding your own business is enough.

Learning to mind your own business may seem, perhaps, a small matter, but it is not, and it matters on many levels. The proclivities of schizophrenia oftentimes throw me into a perceived existential crisis with ample associated paranoia. After all, paranoia is common to my profile. But after living with schizophrenia for quite some time, decades now at that, I have learned it's many facets and I have gleaned a few coping means. One such learned imperative is minding my own business.

Living in a psychotic state, for me, usually includes an associated paranoia. Of course, the paranoia rests on my prevailing cognitive distortions. The enigma of paranoia, in schizophrenia that is, entails its perceived interpersonal conundrum. For a paranoid psychosis proceeds primarily in the interpersonal realm of life. In other words, if no one is about, an acute paranoia will not usually distress, unless of course that is, I am ruminating about perceived potential future difficulties; but again, those being in the interpersonal realm.

A paranoid psychosis plays an act among others. Prior to learning its wiles, my paranoia was once disabling. When paranoid, and lacking my now-internalized coping skills, it would substantially inhibit my ability to function—right down to capably buttering my own bread. A paranoid psychosis is exhibited on many metacognitive levels. The underlying schema of paranoid psychosis involves me wrestling with my own thoughts and perceptions while simultaneously trying to discern the verbiage, gestures, and actions of others. A paranoid psychosis inevitably includes an unhealthy cognitive occupancy regarding the intents and purposes of others. While amid my paranoia, I used to incessantly wrestle with the motives of others, e.g., were others out to get me or slight me in some obvious or not so obvious manner? After years of not fully understanding the matrix of paranoia, I finally crested and garnered a means of coping.

One such primary coping method that I gleaned from my paranoia is minding my own business. Specifically, it is not that I do not infer any sort of social isolation or a lack of interpersonal interaction, rather, minding my own business involves an adaptive sort of micro-level coping. I have learned to primarily manage that which relates to my social immediacy. In a way, I have retreated from sweeping global generalizations, especially regarding universal notions of human nature. Such macro preoccupations, I have found, foment my chances for possible paranoia. For example, paranoia may follow from the macro conclusion that some people are inherently rude, apathetic, and lacking in a degree of empathy. From such a global conclusion, my paranoia may ensue. On the other hand, however, I have learned to mind my own business, specifically on a micro interpersonal level, that is, managing direct small-scale interactions before me. In this way, I have reduced the scaling of my judgments and I now rather prefer minding my own business; that is, that which relates to me directly. I still experience paranoia, and at many different intensities. I confess, it's a terrible experience when florid. Its loneliness chokes. But, over time, I have learned the lesson of minding my own business.

Why is minding my own business essential in the context of schizophrenia and also for my greater life as a whole? Paranoid psychosis comes arm in arm with concern about the motives of others. Paranoia squarely places itself between me and you. When experiencing psychotic paranoia prior to my enhanced coping ability, I was constantly trying to read into the words and behaviors of others. In fact, I was consumed with trying to get accurate data concerning the intents and purposes of others.

I have learned the coping skill of minding my own business. I do not concern myself with your business or that of anyone else in my proximity. I have learned there is no way to penetrate the interpersonal surface to decipher another's will. In fact, I have learned that my ultimate conclusions regarding the intentions of others will be entirely substantiated by my own will, or, in other words, I will find evidence for the motives of others that is entirely based on what I am looking for.

If I seek kindness, I will find evidence in support of it. If I seek malevolence, according to my intent, this too I will find evidence for. So in the end, deciphering the intentions of others becomes a total wash, a waste of energy and, mostly, a matter of personal projection.

On the other hand, minding my own business supports ample ability to cope. No longer do I try to decode the behaviors of others; rather, I focus on my behavior, my speech, my values, and my business. The intentions of others I now take with a grain of salt, because the vibrations of others are entirely reflections of my own presenting psychology. Minding my own business shifts the onus from the other to the self. Self I have control over, others I certainly do not.

Beyond its utility in coping with schizophrenia, I have found minding my own business to be a terrific complement to life external to schizophrenia and coping with it. Minding your own business, that is, focusing on your own conduct and words, removes undo personal preoccupation regarding others. We will never be able to see another's mind like looking under the hood of a car. This being the case, I have found the interpersonal veneer to more than sufficient for allowing me to deduce, and induce, life's meanings (a positive life meaning included). Further, allow me to assume that you may be like me in the following regard: It is my preference to conduct my own business with a high degree of autonomy and liberty. I certainly do not favor another individual unnecessarily meddling in my occupation and vocation. So, in the end, I think it best that we each tend to our own personal gardens. Where the soil may be shared, we will commune; otherwise, our spheres shall share no overlap (comfortably so). Schizophrenia taught me the value of minding my own business—to tend to my own garden. Thus far, this internalized value has harvested a good crop.

Chapter 7

Life Includes Psychological Darkness

Lesson—Have no fear of the dark.

Straight to point, life exists at times with a constituent psychological darkness and this applies to you, me, and everyone else. If we live beyond our existential innocence, be it for 10 years or 90, we have an awareness of the suffering and challenges faced by everyone. Never in my life have I met a soul with an authentic persistent cheerfulness. Sadness, depression, anxiety, fear, anger, and irritability, at times, invade us all. I find this unanimous. But how do we put such psychological struggles in perspective and integrate them healthily?

Schizophrenia has provided ample personal psychological toil and hardship. But please, I implore you to spare me empathic concern, for as you well know, this is certainly not unique to me. At one time, my world certainly seemed to be fixed as my nemesis, adversary, and evil consort. My life has never been as dark and terrifying as when my insight was extremely limited; but, like all matters, this too did pass.

I still experience psychosis, by degree, frequency, and temporality. Despite such perceptions, however, I have learned to manage my behavior, speech, and conduct so as not to act out on psychotic ideation. Psychosis remains an able psychological force, but I have disabled its primary and vicious bite. Psychosis may persist, but I have diminished its consequences, and through a holistic perspective, I have largely stopped it ability to be a certain fixed malevolent ontology. Nevertheless, psychosis persists in its psychological pestering and occasional bites.

Yes, psychosis continues to offer dark perceptions. In large part, I have learned to mitigate these. Long ago, I decided that schizophrenia was not going to ruin my life. This was a conscious and deliberate decision. Once decided, this was the foundation to my recovery. I educated myself about schizophrenia so I could best manage it. Regarding the many variables constituent to schizophrenia, I learned about why symptoms occur and how to combat such impositions. The sum total of all I know regarding schizophrenia I term as "insight." In my opinion, insight is the global variable that guides our recovery, stability, and ultimately our sanity. Now, when I experience symptoms, the depth of my insight allows me to focus on inherent solutions. I have learned that each and every symptom of schizophrenia is indeed followed by a correlated solution. Insight is not an end-state. Insight is developmental and never-ending. Insight includes my full cache of solutions to each and every symptom. Insight is my life preserver.

I have personally negotiated a detente with my psychological armament, and this truce has diminished its darkness. I have integrated such psychological suffering into my more global psychology. Certainly, this has not always been the case. Psychological suffering now abides within my global schema, but it assuredly does not exist singularly. It plays alongside psychological light too.

From my own experiences with psychological despair, I have learned that we all go through periods of bleakness, not just simply "woe is me." At times, life is no picnic, and I think this applies universally. No one traverses without significant adversity, or, more specifically, adversities in the plural form. As a mental health talk therapist, this notion has been reinforced. As a student of life, this notion has become obvious.

I no longer fear psychological suffering. Because of my experience, I have learned many life lessons, including resilience and the art of the bounce back. Suffering is inevitable, but what do we glean from its appropriations?

Dark times are not solo ventures. The dark is only dark because we understand its binary, that being, the light. I find that many of life's inherent variables reside on a sort of spectrum. Accordingly, I find my generalized emotional status as being capably placed on such a spectrum. When someone greets us in passing and asks us, "How are you doing?" we will most often respond in kind, and, in a polite knee-jerk manner, say something the likes of "I am well, and you?" This is a superficial sort of reflexive emotional analysis. When regarding the dark versus light spectrum, I am not referencing such flippant statements, as are so often customary and exemplary of cordial interpersonal politeness, rather, I am referring to a visceral evaluation of my current emotional status. I intend an authentic sort of contextual emotional status, including all things considered. Of course, I have experienced some dark and testing times with my psychosis, but such a story does not entirely end in the dark, absent a soothing sort of light.

I view psychological lightness according to the emotional variable known as euthymia. Euthymia is a clinical psychological term referencing a certain sort of emotional neutrality. It is neither depression nor elation, but rather the intermediary. Euthymia is clinically considered normative and healthy. The manner in which euthymia works is as follows: We begin with the given of a euthymic mood, which is a neutral sort of emotional state. Whilst amid euthymia, and given the context of time passing, when good things in one's life are factored, a euthymic mood may modulate to a sense of joy or happiness. For example, perhaps your child is born or you get a job or a promotion. Or perhaps you are invited to a family picnic and have a good time. Maybe you see a loved one succeed in some manner, perhaps they graduate. When such life items occur, a state of underlying euthymia will modulate towards positive feelings for a time. This, to me, is the psychological light. It is a natural sense of emotional positivity directly in response to a perceived positive life occurrence. Once the positivity passes, returning again to euthymia is the emotionally healthy course. Conversely, when in a euthymic mood and an adverse life event ensues, for example, a relationship squabble, the passing of a loved one, a personal health scare, employment misfortune, or perhaps a minor motor vehicle accident, in response or reflexively, one's mood will again modulate from euthymia to an acute negative sort of experienced emotion. For example, sadness, anxiety, fear, worry, and concern may follow. Nevertheless, I see such an emotional response to life's offerings as a healthy sort of constituent emotional life. Once the adverse life event passes, over time, one's mood will again modulate back to euthymia. From such a baseline status of euthymia, the emotional cycles will repeat again. As an emotional baseline, euthymia is healthy. From this base, healthy emotions will then follow according to the offerings of life events. For me, the psychological light entails resting in euthymia. From here, I remain hopeful for good fortune in life. I do not seek happiness. I seek euthymia.

I think it is difficult to enjoy lighted times without an appreciation of the dark. Psychological distress provides a necessary contrast to psychological appreciation. Psychological dark does not exist in a vacuum though. It resides on a spectrum of illumination and contrast. To endure tough times is to know frivolity. The inverse of this applies as well. The canvas of life bandies between dark and light and concordantly in all shades and illuminations. It is this spectrum that I have come to realize. It is the spectrum that I have come to appreciate.

Once we move beyond our initial life innocence, life can certainly no longer come with the exclusive expectation of solely great and terrific times. Schizophrenia has reinforced this cognizance. Long ago, I forbade illusions of a persistent happiness. In its place followed an appreciation of the wholesome grandeur that is characteristic of life. I can certainly appreciate happiness, but difficult times also teach and inform. Difficult times forge character and allow us to be our best version. We all need ease at times, and this I acknowledge. But I do not harbor illusions of a persistent gladness amid an unabated sort of life picnic. Rather, I have come to appreciate the wholesome life spectrum and I expect no other way.

It is recognition of the spectrum that is the life lesson. I harbor no false notions of a persistent light and I harbor no false notions of avoiding darkened and trying times altogether. With such a perspective, I have learned the value of an emotional stability, void of regular emotional hyperbole. My emotional acuities are no longer pervasive and I take life much more in stride, with a casual acceptance. I now rather prefer a more balanced emotional life of nuance, and I have schizophrenia to thank for this.

Chapter 8

Cognitive Distortions

Lesson—Boy, do cognitive distortions exist.

Dr. Aaron Beck should receive all the credit for his groundbreaking work in cognitive psychology. In fact, he is known as the "father of cognitive therapy". Dr. Beck's seminal work in elucidating underlying cognitive distortions is brilliant. Sadly, Dr. Beck recently passed at age 100. His legacy and work are secured and his kindness remembered.

Schizophrenia instructed me well regarding cognitive distortions. Cognitive distortions involve our thinking. Cognitive distortions are characterized by the various erroneous manners in which we may think about ourselves and our external world. Cognitive distortions facilitate personal suffering, whether this be mild or significant. Such suffering follows from our potentially skewed observations of ourselves and the world around us. Cognitive distortions are defined as thinking errors, and many such errors have been identified and classified. Such cognitive distortions include, for example, black-and-white thinking, over-generalization, selective abstraction, all-or-nothing thinking, jumping to conclusions, and catastrophizing. Beyond these, further types of cognitive distortions have been identified and classified. Cognitive distortions are problematic; however, once we can identify such distortions in our thinking, we can then move towards a healthier life perspective. The good news is that, once cognitive distortions are internally recognized, they are entirely remediable. With such mental correction, suffering is reduced.

Prolifically, many of the symptoms of schizophrenia are directly traceable to underlying cognitive distortions. Schizophrenia is a primary thought disorder. Cognitive distortions are part and parcel to such a thought disorder. Identifying and remedying cognitive distortions has greatly improved my attitude, behaviors, and life in general. Understanding the often automatic errors in our thinking, both in those with schizophrenia and also in people without it, can reduce personal suffering and enhance a healthy life perspective. Cognitive distortions often lack the required nuance essential to our thinking.

Psychosis, in general, is supported by personal beliefs coaxed by cognitive distortions. I view psychosis as a form of cognitive distortion, but even further, I see psychosis as cognitive distortion plus some zest (or cognitive distortion amid ample hyperbole). Psychosis moves one beyond mere distortion to a blurry and nearly imperceptible type of avant-garde visual grounding. It is distortion, further intensified and amplified.

Cognitive distortions, amid innumerable types and admixtures, can facilitate psychosis. There is a clear distinction regarding cognitive distortion in schizophrenia versus cognitive distortion exclusive to schizophrenia. In schizophrenia, ample cognitive distortion can support psychosis. In those absent a mental illness, however, cognitive distortion certainly can and does occur, but such distortions will not remotely approach psychosis. Rather, the results of such cognitive distortions will result in a sort of skewing of perception, including, perhaps, an unhealthy or maladaptive perception of oneself or the world around them. Indeed, cognitive distortion external to mental illness presents, however, it can be found with a much greater sort of subtlety. Nevertheless, and most assuredly, cognitive distortions unequivocally support cognitive psychosis, and very directly at that.

Cognitive distortions are maladaptive or unhealthy internalized means of coping with the challenges we are met with in life. Cognitive distortions can support our perceptions of the world and across various subjectivities. Rather than a sort of tempered rationality, cognitive distortions will induce highly skewed perceptions of the world.

For example, in the cognitive distortion of black-and-white thinking, its derivative entails seeing the world in a certain dichotomy; either as entirely one particular way or another, i.e., entirely black or entirely white. Such a perspective lacks a needed nuance, the availability of shades of gray. In my case, when I was both psychotic and paranoid, I was viewing other people as wholly and inherently persecutory, punitive, and directive of ill-intent. I saw people as having no personal nuance. Once identifying my distortion, I arrived with an accordant solution; that being that the more cognitively adaptive conclusions of each human had a combination of personality traits, including many inherent positive qualities. Ultimately, I ditched my distorted black-and-white thinking and this, in turn, reduced my psychosis and paranoia. Consequently, I assumed an improved and nuanced perspective, resulting in improved functioning and adaptivity.

Overgeneralization is another example of a classified cognitive distortion. Overgeneralization involves inaccurate and grossly sweeping overgeneralizations. In my case, for example, when I was both psychotic and paranoid, my character judgments of others were highly flawed. If I observed a single act of human malevolence, I took this recognition and then applied this as a judgment, in a sweeping manner, to all people. Further, if someone was entirely disrespectful, I again would embrace its occurrence and then apply such a quality to all. Accordingly, I made the inaccurate overgeneralization that all people were inherently disrespectful. Such a personal cognitive distortion supported my psychosis and paranoia because I entirely viewed all people as having such negative traits. Therefore, I became paranoid regarding the actions and intentions of all others. Ultimately, I identified my underlying overgeneralization regarding the innate qualities of human beings. I corrected my distortion in favor of a more accurate depiction of people; this being that each of us is unique and are made up of a unique combination of traits and personalities. In many ways, cognitive distortions flourish in schizophrenia. Once such distortions can be identified and then corrected, the symptoms of schizophrenia can diminish, significantly so. Cognitive distortions exist at the edge of tempered reason and tip toe into the "barely rational" or the obviously "irrational". When someone passionately acts with an enthusiastic sort of obvious irrationality, you can be sure that such behavior rests on cognitive distortion.

Dr. Beck's work elucidated various types of cognitive distortions. Again, his work here is seminal, enduring, and brilliant. Dr. Beck was also the pioneer of cognitive behavioral therapy (CBT), the oft-agreed-upon consensus modality in many mental health circles, realms, and applications. For me, in my practice as a mental health therapist, I frequently use cognitive behavioral therapy. CBT, as its name suggests, draws attention to one's thinking, i.e., the cognitive, and also to one's behaviors, i.e., the behavioral. With a focus on maladaptation, or otherwise on detrimental coping skills and unhealthy behaviors, an individual's underlying problems can be identified and this can be followed by pertinent solutions. CBT is very practical and solution-focused. CBT is often considered a "best practice" modality for many types of mental illnesses. Best practice means that a certain modality or therapeutic approach has been confirmed as effective according to its associated research. In other words, it has been proven to be effective.

Dr. Beck also pioneered cognitive behavioral therapy for psychosis (CBTp) by applying the cognitive behavioral realms to schizophrenia. CBTp is considered a best practice in the treatment of schizophrenia. It simply has the same principles as CBT, but applied to issues in schizophrenia. Dr. Beck's legendary work spans the full spectrum of mental health issues, and schizophrenia is certainly included.

Personally, in my own psychology and its application to my issues with psychosis, I can now identify many inherent distortions.

Ever intriguingly, each singular symptom of schizophrenia can oftentimes be directly correlated to an underlying cognitive distortion. Psychosis is a significantly blurred vision of the world, substantiated, at least in part, by prevailing cognitive distortions. If I am paranoid, I can trace its etiology to a cognitive distortion. If I am feeling persecuted, it again can be traced to another type of distortion. If I engage in existential hyperbole, yet another form of distortion. I have discovered that my psychosis lies fully on the foundation of cognitive distortions.

Psychosis, I find, is not a singular distortion, but is more of an intermingled mixed bag of several. Adding together a handful of cognitive distortions, plus distortions with power and zest (i.e., intensity), plus distortions that are "fixed" (or persistent over time), and adding distortions that are most convincing based on quality, and the result will be proximate to a prevailing psychosis. After all, psychosis is a state of mind supported by beliefs and perceptions. Such is the perfect cocktail for an emerging psychosis.

Make no mistake, cognitive distortions present also in others, beyond schizophrenia, as well. Cognitive distortions present in mental illness and in others without a diagnosable mental illness. Underlying cognitive distortions can be found in all sorts of cognitive behavioral presentations; be it anger, depression, life adjustments, or just plain human irrationality. All can be understood by underlying distortions. Even the most healthily adjusted of us all will at times succumb to cognitive irrationalities and associated behaviors. Cognitive distortions are par for the course, and we all dawdle on the course. Mind you, cognitive distortions are evident in all, at least in part, by degree and intensity.

After recognizing one's cognitive distortions, then follows remedy and amelioration. In my case, when I recognize a cognitive distortion wreaking havoc, I remediate. Once I remediate the symptom or problem, it dissipates, like an inert gas vanishing into thin air, and I am once again renewed with a sense of restorative mental clarity and relief.

Schizophrenia has induced regular cognitive distortions into my prevailing psychology. For me, such irrationalities are common. But, once identified, and I identify them often, better times and experiences ensue. At once, I am altogether ignorant regarding cognitive distortions, and such ignorance has caused me much suffering, potentially undo suffering at that. When pursuing my master's degree in social work, I learned a lot regarding psychology, including the body of work of Dr. Aaron Beck. For me, initially identifying my underlying cognitive distortions took me some time and practice. Firstly, I had to learn them as to their inherency or common templates. Once I understood the various distortions, I then could begin to apply them to my personal experiences, and, boy, at times such cognitive distortions resonated exuberantly. Additionally, in a professional capacity, my understanding of cognitive distortions was further enhanced and reinforced. I use the CBT modality often. In a general manner, I have now been thinking about cognitive distortions for some 15 years, both in relation to my own psychology and relating to the psychology of others. Learning the basics of cognitive distortions does not require any sort of exceptional capacity; rather, learning the basics of cognitive distortions is highly (and easily) accessible. In a very direct manner, in my own psychology, I use the teachings of CBT for my own betterment.

I have, in a sense, become my own best therapist and this too can follow for you. It simply takes some learning and a little practice. In my professional practice, I often encourage others to do similarly; that is, to become their own best therapist. Such a self-efficacy is readily attainable.

I find it most ironic that the most irrational of all psychological mechanisms, otherwise known as schizophrenia, has taught me the lesson of tempered rationalism. Such rationalism becomes my goal absent of unnecessary distortions or associated symptoms. From the consequences of schizophrenia has followed the lesson of steady reason.

Chapter 9

"Dark" Humor

Lesson—If requisite, dark humor is copacetic and palliative.

Humor in life is an essential coping mechanism. Sometimes, we laugh rather than cry. We all go through trying times, and that it is certain for everyone. If you think you may be singularly suffering amid life, I assure you that it is a universal experience. Suffering is global. It is only the manner in which we suffer that differs from person to person.

Long ago, I learned that suffering is a part of life. I also came to an impasse and acceptance that I cannot (or will not) avoid suffering. In the end, I have concluded that it's natural to suffer. Further, with acceptance once it occurs, it provides lessons. With acceptance, a layer of suffering is removed. Without accepting suffering, its characteristic doubles accordingly in terms of its intensity and occupancy. Accepting your own suffering cuts down its severity, to a certain degree.

If suffering is not psychologically integrated, its characteristic will be an even further burden. Denial of suffering exacerbates its timbre and inflames its temperament. In my instance, I learned to integrate suffering as a given. If it announces its presence, I welcome its onset. It scares me not, and is radically copacetic.

Quite simply put, as humans, our primary motive is to attain pleasure and avoid pain. This framing squares nicely with my acceptance of the latter. Once I accept the premise of suffering then I can advance to its expulsion so that I can move in the direction of pleasure on the spectrum. As an aside, please recognize the pleasure–pain dynamic as a spectrum. For without one the other is disqualified, and vice versa.

Suffering shows in its presentation, degree, novelty, and banality. Its characteristic, too, can be creative and prolific. Every day, a new form of suffering can be observed or experienced. Therefore, given the premise of the acceptance of suffering, how do I facilitate its understanding?

Schizophrenia is a primary "thought disorder", in contrast to primary "mood disorders", although certain overlaps can be found. Over the course of living with schizophrenia, via its primary cognitive traits, schizophrenia has induced innumerable ideations for my observing mind to consider and evaluate. Schizophrenia, characteristically, is cognitively provocative. Living with schizophrenia over these many decades, I have had ideas aplenty. Schizophrenia has induced delusions of all sorts, from A to Z, from the metaphysical to the common, from the theological to the humanistic, and from the dark to the light. For example, I once believed that I had been abducted by aliens in my sleep and taken to another planet to dwell. For days, I walked in the community believing that I was on another planet, amongst aliens disguised as humans. Per the persecutory, on other occasions, and these delusions lasted for months, I believed to be surveilled by the government, by satellite technology, for reasons of malicious intent. This persecutory delusion was brutal and perhaps the worst of them all. From this generalized delusion came many associated delusional offshoots. Another time, when I was psychiatrically hospitalized, I believed, in the night, that I was taken from my room and lobotomized. In another example, I believed I would soon be reincarnated and my next time around in life I would be born in Taiwan. I was thoroughly convinced of this for days. As for another, I remember believing that others could move their mind to any location desired in their body rather than it being solely in one's head, and I consequently had bizarre perceptions when interacting with others. For example, I remember talking to someone's elbow because I thought they moved their mind to their mid arm. Such delusions have been very robust and, in terms of such novel types of ideas, I have run the cognitive gamut. Such delusions are but a very brief listing of a greater whole. Admittedly, the vast majority of my delusions have been clinically characterized as persecutory, but certainly not all of them. Across the spectrum of ideas, schizophrenia has had a vast cast of characters and I have necessarily considered the many by-products.

Ideas with psychotic timbres have long percolated in my psychology. Schizophrenia has induced delusions of all types, including, by diagnostic category, the persecutory (by the majority), the religious, and the bizarre. Over the course of my schizophrenia, I have had a few grandiose cognitions as well, but these are countable on one hand and have been temporally fleeting. One such grandiose idea was also accompanied by religiosity. Religious delusions are often common in schizophrenia. I experienced the robust delusion of morphing from a human into a godly entity and I found myself, by perception, surrounded by others who I thought were my prophets. Further, regarding grandiosity, I have had many delusions of knowing numerable globally prominent people, including the famous and the influential. Regarding my experiences with the grandiose, all such delusions have been marked by temporal brevity. Further, all such experienced grandiose delusions unanimously morphed into delusions of persecution. For many with schizophrenia, however, grandiose delusions can be euphoric and invigorating, and for some during the experience, no trace of felt detriment is immediately experienced. In my professional capacity, I have seen such a grandiose congruence many times. Nevertheless, such experiences are delusional and, in a greater perspective, unhealthy. Concurrently, regarding my own felt grandiose delusions, few as they may have been, they certainly also had a sense of agreeability, and were less characterized by somberness.

The conglomeration of certain cognitions will coalesce, at times, into the form of a psychosis. Amid this psychosis, perceptions have great potential for resulting delusions. I have become necessarily skilled at mitigation. Over my many years with schizophrenia, I have learned many acquisitive coping skills, whether they are cognitively or behaviorally derivative. When psychosis emerges acutely, I consider it to be when the proverbial "rubber meets the road." When psychosis acutely provokes, coping must immediately rush to the forefront. In terms of acute coping, for example, over the years, I have identified many reactionary cognitive affirmations; in fact, I keep a written running list of such cognitive coping statements. Additionally, for when psychosis greets, I have also learned supportive behaviors to ride out the acute psychosis. For example, I maintain healthy lifestyle habits, including a healthy diet, abstaining from all drugs and alcohol, good sleep hygiene, ample stress management, and regular exercise. I have also learned to manage my speech characteristics. When amid psychotic thoughts, I pay close attention to what I say to others so as to not speak erratically or out of proper social context. Psychosis can make someone say bizarre things. I learned long ago to manage to avoid erratic speech. According to such a cognitive–behavioral approach, once psychosis creeps in, I've already learned to mitigate it. Such mitigation is my recourse to a presenting psychosis.

Nevertheless, psychosis often comes with an ample bout of suffering. I have learned the value of humor, but more specifically a type of "dark" humor. I consider dark humor the ability to laugh at something painful, perhaps even horrifying, troublesome, or scary. I consider dark humor the ability to laugh at that which is not patently funny.

Persecutory delusions are my worst symptom of all. Schizophrenia has yielded its fair share of these, and a little more. Believing in life as a fixed metaphysical adversary can be daunting. But, like all my conjurings, I have learned this too shall eventually pass. With each passing, I have learned the skill of a retrospective reframing inclusive of the tang of a dark sense of humor. I have learned that psychosis can be psychologically painful, however, when thinking about a past psychosis, maintaining a morose reflection provides me no psychological relief. Rather, once in a safe space and temporal distance, I can view my psychotic ideas with a different sort of psychological lens, including the appreciation of humor, dark it may be.

When I now reflect on my past psychotic cognitions, I now often retort to them with a chuckle. These robust ideas of mine oftentimes leave a psychological residue, if not remaining an entrenched life memory. I have been asked if I remember my experiences with psychosis. It may surprise you to learn that I certainly do, and often in great detail. In fact, I find psychosis to be sometimes surreal. Given the novelty and uniqueness to psychosis, it oftentimes leaves an enthusiastic etching in my memory. Its impositions are often robust and, consequently, they are most difficult to forget.

Psychosis transacts across my intellect with considerable power and consequently memories linger. I have learned, however, that holding on to powerful adverse memories does me no favors. I have learned to reframe my psychosis, tinged with humor.

When I now reflect on such once painful cognitions, I do so amid a dispositional humor. If you follow my meaning, powerful life memories, when viewed in retrospect, can hold new potential perspectives. Many of my psychotic ideas are so otherworldly that, upon reflection, or upon a triggered memory, I must in part guffaw. I now look at these once painful times with a sort of psychological frivolity. I will think, "Man, that was bizarre," followed by a cracked smile. Or, I will say, "Holy cow, how can that have been possible?" with a glint in my eye. For example, when I was having a psychotic episode, I believed I knew many prominent and influential people and celebrities. Of course, it was entirely delusional because I had no such interpersonal contact. It all occurred within my psychotic mind. When I now reflect on all my purported and perceived relationships with famous people, it now amuses me, substantially so. Such conjurings seem so entirely bizarre, and so entirely impossible, that I must otherwise scoff with a grin, if not outright laugh.

I used to feel that it was inappropriate to laugh at my own psychosis because, in a general way, it is a very serious topic. But actually, it is not necessarily the case, especially in retrospect. I now find it healthy to laugh at certain inflicted pains. Again, humor lessens the load, seemingly at all times. If I am so bold as to say, even further, that if you cannot laugh at your troubles, significant and ample coping will be inhibited. It is healthy to reframe pain to something else. I now find it permissible to laugh at my past hardships, at least intrapsychically. If a hardship has passed, we do not need to continue to carry its emotional baggage unnecessarily. Once in retrospect, new perspectives avail themselves.

Schizophrenia has induced its fair share of personal psychological disruption, but I have to look at past events anew, and with a sort of humorous repose. Schizophrenia has taught me the given of psychological pain. Schizophrenia has also taught me to crack a smile upon its passing. It has taught me the value of humor when coping with hardship, and I now apply this to my life from a more general perspective. I thank schizophrenia for this lesson on humor, dark though it may be.

Chapter 10

It Is Wise Not to Compare

Lesson—Find your own Tao and the rest
is beyond comparison.

Allow me to suggest that we are not playing poker. If we were amid chips and dealers, a comparison of our hands would be pertinent. The disparities between aces and deuces would apply. While the game of life may ring with similitude to a hand of cards, I propose that it is not, and that this is not a minor difference, but rather a radical one.

After many initial missteps in managing my schizophrenia, I found myself in an outpatient mental health program called Continuing Day Treatment (CDT). CDT, a now defunct modality, but similarly replaced by the Personalized Recovery Oriented Service (PROS), was a mental health program that spanned the entire day. Arrival at the program began at 8 am, and lingerers could be found at 3 pm. Personally, I attended CDT Monday through Friday from about 9 am to 2 pm. At the conclusion of my CDT program, I would often head north to an adjunct mental health program with the characteristics of a mental health social club. The social club opened around 2 pm and would finish the day (with some variations) depending on the scheduled activities. The home base of the social club had features such as a pool table (my favorite respite), board games, card games, books, a big-screen TV with an ample cache of the old DVDs, as well as arts and crafts, as well as many other items and activities.

CDT had classes throughout the day and I could choose among a few of them. The classes were psychoeducational, social, and/or related to skill building. Each class ran for about 50 minutes and each was instructed by mental health professional, primarily social workers. Such classes included examples such as "Medication Education", "Stress Management", "Current Events", "Building Skills", and many more. Over the course of the day, I would attend some three to four classes and partake of a one-dollar lunch menu and break.

The social club was staffed by mental health professionals, and also our peers, those being, like others with mental illness, now recovered. The social club too always had groups, but they were entirely social in character, ranging from bingo, to current events, to learning yoga or journaling, and everything between. Further, the social club would also go out into the community, going to movies, community events, bowling, shopping malls, sporting events, and other wholesome community activities. Ten of us would pile into a minivan and head to our destination.

This combination of CDT and associated social club occupied my time from early morning to at least pre-dinner time. I did this combination of activities for some nine months. During these nine months, I worked on my general mental health recovery. The combination of the programs gave me the time to work on gaining stability. I really did not have fun during that time, but I knew that I needed to engage, establish some structure to my time and day, and especially to learn about schizophrenia and its many angles. I learned tremendous amounts regarding schizophrenia and other major mental illnesses. Further, I learned troves from my peers, including some who had lived with mental illness for decades. At the time, I was a mere newbie, so I absorbed all I could. I think I learned more from my peers than the classes, but it was a close call.

For a while, this combination was my life's activity. In many ways, this time was crucial for me. It provided me a psychoeducation and to this day I view psychoeducation as paramount to recovery. At the time, I did not realize just how essential the education I was absorbing was. I did not enjoy the program much, but it was the very best structured activity I could have possibly chosen, although it was only due to suggestion and encouragement that I initially attended. In these programs, I learned the ropes regarding all matters of mental health. I found an inadvertent peer group by manner of common engagement. While I attended, admittedly, I was not enthused. Retrospectively, I now know that this temporality was the absolute foundation that I needed to recover. Further, my involvement eventually led me to become a "peer counselor" (a social worker at CDT thought I would make a good peer counselor). I eventually applied for this paid position, was hired, and this began my work in the field of mental health. Ironically, I never would have worked in mental health if not for attending CDT. After all, my bachelor's degree was in broadcasting. I had vocationally dabbled in broadcasting, but I had been run off the tracks by schizophrenia. Turns out that this confluence of events eventually became a boon; it turns out that I had a hearty distaste for broadcasting. This change in vocation was exactly what I needed. It seems to me highly serendipitous. To this day, I chuckle about such a haphazard vocational change. Never in my life would have I ever considered the mental health field were it not for my schizophrenia. This was a powerful example to me of serendipity, and one I will not soon forget. Sometimes life's adversities turn out for the best.

My life was dull and my future opportunities seem blocked from all avenues. My future, to my then naïve eyes, looked very unpromising and I was scared. There I sat in a CDT class; I took in my surroundings and absorbed my then gestalt. I had no money, no occupational prospects, and I was very much a lost soul. I looked at my then environment and intellectually shuddered. My life appeared bleak and my future prospects looked grim. I felt like my life was at a proverbial dead-end.

After fully appreciating my situation in life, I then looked to my peers and similar others. As you may understand, according to a surface appraisal, the comparisons were unfavorable, including according to material standards. Many of my friends were doing much otherwise compared to my own daily activities. Please know, I now know such comparisons are absurd, given schizophrenia's life lesson. But apparently, my friends were, well, appearing to be successful relative to my own lack therein. I found much the same comparisons with family members of my age group, including cousins and a sibling. I felt bottomed out. Others seemed, by a perceived ridiculous degree, to be meeting lofty goals while I viewed myself, by comparison, as mired and inadequate. How naïve I was. I lacked wisdom. I lacked perspective. I lacked life experience.

I now know from living my life for these many decades, along with the intrinsic knowledge of an associated schizophrenia, that lives are beyond comparison, extraordinarily so. Life is not meant to be compared with your neighbor, grocer, or waiter. Each person has their own singular path through life. I personally reference this unique path with the Eastern philosophic term, "Tao". Tao, as defined, means "the path." Tao is the recognition that each individual will have their own unique path across their lifespan. No two personal Taos will match, as each is unique to each and all. In addition to an inherent singular life path, Tao also suggests an associated sort of underlying disposition and temperament. Such a characteristic entails a sort of personal balance across the lifespan. Such a balance is often generically referred to as "yin–yang." Tao infers traveling your own unique path amid a sense of dispositional composure. Further, Tao is the dynamic of one's path traveled amid one's associated disposition. Such an interplay is the essence of Tao.

We each have our own unique Tao. For some, life adversities come early, and for others, perhaps later. Sometimes, life will be upended in youth, while for others it happens in their later years. Life simply deals unique variables and challenges to each person across radically differentiated temporalities. We all experience life adversities. Regarding our Tao, from each life adversity follows an allowance for personal choice. Each instance of life adversity qualifies as a veritable "fork in the road." Such adversities can ultimately urge us to forge new grounds.

The correlated lesson to not compare myself with others entails the recognition of each person's unique Tao with an unequivocally associated singular brilliance. I can deeply appreciate,
and also marvel at, your traveled path. I have learned that each
person's Tao is uniquely sublime and concordant with a sort of
shimmering light. But this reality can only be appreciated beyond personal comparisons. I have learned an appreciation for
your Tao, as well as my own. Schizophrenia taught me to appreciate the myriads of unique and fascinating Taos. At one time, I
was naïve to such an impressive sort of individualism. Schizophrenia, however, taught me otherwise, and I am all the better
for it.

As for my own personal Tao, that is, my own path through
life, I offer the following: Personally, I try to remain in the present or the given day. I have come to appreciate unanticipated life
offerings. I do not try to necessarily preconceive my long-term
future, or even too far beyond tomorrow. This is not to say I do
not have goals or plans for tomorrow. I certainly have both.
Rather, I see my Tao as a sort of broader life perspective. It entails embracing not only goals and future planning, but also includes a vision of life that is inclusive to life unexpectedness. I do
not know with any certainty what life will bring today, tomorrow, or in the years ahead. Schizophrenia has taught me this. Life
includes both the expected and the unexpected. Embracing both
is part of my own personal Tao. Further, I do not mean to infer
that all unexpected life occurrences are necessarily detrimental.
At times, unexpected life events may indeed follow as an en-
hancement to life or an asset. Make no mistake, however, life
will offer adversities. These, too, I have come to readily accept.

In the grand scheme, my own Tao includes my personal plans as denominated by certain emergent life challenges or adversities. This Tao of mine serves as my path. My path is as unique as yours. Additionally, my Tao entails enthusiastically embracing the combination of life that includes, not only my plans, but also the inherent spontaneity of life. Although goals certainly remain important, no one can plan ahead for everything. Therefore, I come to a dispositional ease when improvisation may be required. As for the very end of my path, or my Tao, if I reach my later years, of 90 years lived or perhaps beyond, and if all factors align favorably, I hope to be able to sit comfortably on my porch, in my favorite rocking chair with some good company alongside a faithful canine companion. If I am fortunate, in the very end, my Tao will involve such a simple but pleasing scenario. Rocking, I may rest on the laurels of my life' accomplishments. Further yet, I will also embrace what the given day may bring, including further unanticipated life offerings. Simply because my sphere may be reduced to my porch does not mean freedom from yet more adversity. Characteristically, regarding the general concept of Tao, it entails a life flexibility, including the capacity, when needed, to forge new grounds. Tao also implies a sort of dispositional ease which includes taking life however it may come. Tao is graceful. Tao entails an underlying sort of cognitive equanimity, regardless of what life may bring. Tao is never forced and is gentle, like a slight wind. Compare not. Live your own brilliance and your sublime Tao will surely shine.

Chapter 11

Interpersonal Ethics

Lesson—I have never regretted my acts of kindness.

Schizophrenia, very capably, previously and also (at times) in the present, can scare me out of my wits. Psychotic perceptions can be disturbing and wrought with fear. In my case, a primary symptom of mine is persecutory delusions with an associated paranoia. Delusions of persecution are held beliefs that others have a directed ill-intent towards me. Many times, across my time with schizophrenia, I have grappled with delusions of persecution and with the inducement of an ample paranoia. When I am amid a delusion of persecution, I feel that all others in my environment are focused on me, with an eye towards some sort of injurious intent, whether it be emotional, physical, or both. Regarding my feelings that all others in my environment are focused on me, such a delusion is known clinically as "spotlighting". As it infers, spotlighting is the perception of being the primary focus of others, or is otherwise akin to being the center of attention, similar to when someone is performing on stage. Once I learned about the delusion of spotlighting, and with a little time and practice, I came to greatly reduce this such wreaking havoc. I now know such a perception certainly qualifies as a delusion.

Delusions of persecution, supported by the experience of spotlighting, was once terrifying. When I was amid this type of provocative delusion, for example, I came to believe that, not only did those in my immediate social environment want to injure or eliminate me, but also that my family wanted to alienate me. Sometimes, as a recourse, I would pray to God. But, further yet, I would then experience persecutory delusions regarding God. For example, while amid auditory hallucinations, I would hear God's persecutory voice lamenting my very soul as being eternally damned. This combination of all people and God intentionally rejecting me was horrific, especially in the worst of times. I am lucky I survived. Presently, however, my struggles with persecutory delusions have decreased tenfold, and perhaps even further. Secondary to educating myself on general schizophrenia, and on this type of specified delusion, I have gained the requisite insight for tremendous progress. In general, such persecutory delusions in schizophrenia are common hallmarks, and I am certainly not alone in experiencing them. Given such generality, in myself and others, what makes up this complex and conjoined persecutory–paranoid dynamic and why is it so terribly provocative?

I now know my persecutory delusions are entirely predicated on my underlying and presenting cognitive distortions. Yes, this

I know with a certainty, and with this insight, I now cope capably. Regarding this, in the persecutory–paranoid coupling, persecutory delusions are primary and paranoia follows in its wake. Once, this conglomeration pushed me to the brink. This brink included bouts of suicidal ideation. I regularly thought that suicide might be the best option. I felt that the world was against me. In fact, further to this, I thought that others wanted me to commit suicide. I had perceptions of others, including through auditory hallucinations, goading me to commit suicide. I felt entirely alone with absolutely nowhere to turn. My inhibition to suicide was the recurring notion that I just did not have the capacity to annihilate or destroy myself. This ideation preserved me. Additionally, I also had an ever-so-slight remaining sliver of a lighted sense of hope. I did not entirely abandon the hope that my horrific experiences might, at some point, eventually relent or be relieved. This time was brutal for me. Psychosis caused suicidal thought in me and I know it can, also happen in others.

Regarding such brinkmanship, I have learned that many with schizophrenia go through similar experiences; not only with ideas of self-harm, but also perhaps ideas of harm-to-others. Some with schizophrenia, in response to such feelings of persecution, may have the idea of lashing back at others by manner of harm-to-others. In my case, however, my abject direness was directed at myself, and therefore followed my suicidal ideation. I did not have significant ideas of harming others, but, in a way, I can understand such a psychological reaction in others (although without condoning it in the slightest, of course). I think I can understand why harm-to-others may follow as sequela of schizophrenia, but it is so tragic when it occurs. To this day, I continue to experience the persecutory–paranoid confluence. But, over these many years, I have learned to subjugate its psychotic bark, if not its bite. No longer do I experience suicidal ideation, nor have I in many, many years.

A bit further regarding the persecutory–paranoid gestalt, when amid this acute coupling, my anxiety heightens. In a very direct and intense manner, my perceptions are that everyone in my environment are out to get me (for some enigmatic reason). I feel that others want me expelled from mutual company and will exact on me to achieve this shared goal of my extinction. With these delusional perceptions of being persecuted, along with a heightened anxiety, flows an ample paranoia. This psychological communion is like a beast.

With improved insight, I no longer have ample fret or worry, because I know I can cope with such cognitive provocations, and I do so with a calm emotional ease. I have tamed this particular lion, and have further gleaned its associated life lesson. Amid persecutory–paranoid experiences, at one time in my life, I would feel alone and desperate. But fortunately, I persisted, and like all matters, these things too (mostly) passed. In trying to learn to manage these once-disturbing experiences, a lesson had to be learned before remediation and relaxation followed.

It is firstly important to understand the underlying psychology, that is, the reality of perceptions of a sort of persecution directed at my existence and to my face. Once, they were uncomfortable indeed; however, I have now debunked these perceptions and acquired the necessary life lesson and its associated skill.

It may be otherwise obvious, but I have learned to view others according to their unique individualities. Previously, I grouped all people together, in the form of a gang, and attributed to this grouping a unified sort of persecutory intent. I did not see individual characteristics, only attributable group characteristics. Schizophrenia induced this distorted perception. I overgeneralized. I came to learn to dismiss the associated delusion of spotlighting. This insightful combination ultimately qualified my cognitive remediation, ensuring that my behavior followed this lead. I learned to interact with individuals and not groups. I modulated my behavior through a focus on that which I faced rather than admonishing a sweeping overgeneralization that included some sort of malevolent group-think. Regarding group dynamics, I certainly do not ignore altogether, but, rather, I now view the group with a more requisite nuance rather than unnecessary global conclusions. This, in turn, reduced the intensity of my persecutory perceptions and psychosis. I also learned to remain rational amid my behaviors, and to not behave or speak out from a normative social context. Once I learned to deconstruct this type of presenting psychosis, in addition to an exuberant sense of psychological relief and easing, followed further fruits in the form of an associated sort of life lesson.

While in the persecutory–paranoid confluence, I once viewed those in my environment as empowered and my own will as negligent. My perception was entirely misguided. Amid these ideas, I used to obsess about the intents, behaviors, words, and gestures of others in an attempt to decode a cryptic communicable persecution. My locus of control was entirely embedded in others. I would constantly self-dialogue about why I was deserving of such persecution. For after all, I believe myself to be decent and not deserving of ill intent. I would ask, "Why?". This push–pull dynamic finally diminished when I directly shifted the balance of control, from others to myself.

I learned that, in no way, was I in fact deserving of being malevolently mistreated. I learned that rather than deciphering the perceived cryptic behaviors of others, the only behavior I could control was my own. I stopped reading into the behaviors of others and began to accept others based on how they acted towards me. I no longer viewed a kind gesture as a cryptic action of ill intent. I now can accept niceness as niceness. On the other hand, if someone factually and overtly disrespects me, I simply walk in the other direction and ignore them. But, most candidly, I have not recently experienced any such sort of a personal disregard.

In the end, after enduring such experiences, it all eventually passed. Specifically, when I shifted the focus of my control from others to myself, the burden was lifted. I now live according to my internalized values and I behave in kind. I act on my values and not on the possible intentions of others. I live according to my ideals, values, and my expectations. I use these values as my interpersonal conduits. I express my values of love, respect, kindness, empathy, care, humor, manners, and politeness. These are my items of control, and the intentions of others are not. This shift in focus changed my life and my paradigm.

Further, I have found, generally speaking, that my expressed values are often reciprocated, and many times over. I have found no regrets from an extended sort of expressive kindness. Never have I regretted being kind to others. Schizophrenia has taught me to cease my preoccupation with the possible intentions of others and to internalize a respectful code of self-conduct.

Schizophrenia has served as a conduit to an internalized set of benevolent interpersonal values, and occurred due to a tipping of the scale where the onus was placed. This, I find, another sort of amazing irony in my journey with schizophrenia.

Chapter 12

Vocational Creativity

Lesson—Mastering the art of the vocational zigzag.

Schizophrenia has taught me a sense of creativity, and has done so in more than one manner. Schizophrenia can spark creativity in my thinking. Many times, my ideas have perhaps been of a psychotic timbre, but I cannot dispute a corresponding sort of imaginative novelty, including routine non-normative content as such. Beyond my occasional cognitive whimsy, schizophrenia has also taught me to improvise spontaneously, as may be required. Practically, beyond mere cognitive creativity, schizophrenia also has taught me to behaviorally zig rather than zag when needed. In other words, if one life avenue presents a sort of dead-end, I can always look to an alternate route or another avenue. The creativity associative with my schizophrenia has been a most welcome by-product (perhaps the best such side-effect). Specifically, regarding creativity in a very practical realm, I will further elucidate on vocational creativity.

Schizophrenia has disrupted my vocations many times, and in many ways. I have always valued a personal work ethic, so my vocational disruptions triggered in me a certain and significant psychological nagging. I always assumed, from my teen years and beyond, that I would engage in persistent employment, and also have a broader sense of focus on my career. Initially, schizophrenia detonated this concept (and quite capably at that). At once, as a consequence of dealing with recurring bouts of psychosis, when I found myself unemployed, it gnawed terribly on my sensibilities. Due to my long-held vision of work and a career, when I was not working due to my issues with schizophrenia, I felt a sense of failure and entirely discouraged. Schizophrenia tossed my preconceived notions of employment askew, and, at one time, this was psychologically nagging and most troublesome. But according to the associated life lesson regarding vocations, schizophrenia taught me to not overly sweat or worry about such unemployment considerations. Rather, schizophrenia taught me wisdom regarding the art of the ever-aesthetic vocational zigzag, and I am so much the better for it.

For about three years in my early 20s, I was greatly struggling with my generalized mental health recovery and by no means was it yet substantiated. During that time, I was highly symptomatic, including regular psychosis. I had no insight into my illness yet, and it is a small miracle, I think, that I was even working at all. Over the course of this most tumultuous period of time, I worked at several locales. I worked in an Italian deli for some six months. There, I made sandwiches, ran the register, and doled out the dough (literally) as the best home-made breads. After about six months, I was fired and my dismissal was entirely due to my erratic functioning amid my active psychosis. In retrospect, I tried really hard during that time, and, given my yet-untreated schizophrenia, I am proud of my efforts then.

Shortly thereafter, I worked at a Greek restaurant washing dishes. I did this for about two years. The by-products of my labor were a modest monetary sustenance, an achy back from persistently leaning deep into wash basins, and an impressive set of wrinkled hands akin to a set of prunes. During those two years, I was floridly psychotic and the restaurant owners, I wager, could easily gauge my erratic behavior. But, after all, it was of no matter because the owners needed a dishwasher and psychological stability was apparently a secondary requisite! I actually took a lot of pride in this job. Beyond dishes, I also would perform a myriad of kitchen-related activities. After two years of bending over the sinks, my mental health issues became so acute that I was psychiatrically hospitalized and did not return to the restaurant.

During those three years of instability, I worked at a grocery store in the bakery, and of all jobs, if you believe it, I was trained as a cake decorator. I decorated cakes for about a year. To this day, I have a unique sort of expertise regarding cakes by manner of the associated aesthetics. I actually had a lot of fun decorating cakes and it sated both my creativity and my appetite.

Once I recovered from my schizophrenia a handful of years later, I returned to college for graduate school and pursued and obtained my MSW (Master of Social Work). With my MSW, followed by my LMSW (Licensed Master Social Worker), and eventually my LCSW (Licensed Clinical Social Worker) in my back pocket, I continued to dally amid a diverse set of jobs and employers. Sometimes, I left a specific job due to my intruding mental health, and other times I switched things up out of interest for something new or a new intriguing opportunity. I have been in my current vocation and position for around five years.

I have seen many times, in observing others, that oftentimes, career-wise, some are fortunate (at least apparently) and follow a more traditional type of work trajectory, e.g., many years with a single employer, perhaps with intermittent advancements or promotions. For me, however, schizophrenia taught me to pay this more normative trajectory no undue mind. Schizophrenia taught me that necessity is the mother of all invention.

Schizophrenia taught me, that, at the end of the day, financial and emotional sustenance can exist beyond typical career forms. I learned, "Who cares if you have to job hop?". There is no statute regarding changing jobs, regardless of the underlying issues. Further, if it pays the bills then the mission has been accomplished. Further yet, I have found that the generalized labor force is flooded with employment opportunities; if, of course, you are not overly restricting yourself to the types of jobs you may normally pursue. In my case, I have run the gamut, from dishes, to cakes, to talk therapy. When in each (and all) of my positions, I took pride in what I did. I found that none of my vocations were more noble than the rest, and, to this day, I find value in all my once-proffered ventures. I think that I most enjoyed making cakes. In retrospect, I could have parlayed it into a career.

There is one final thing to mention regarding mastering the art of the vocational zigzag. This final nuance entails one of my all-time favorite conceptions, this being what is known as serendipity. Serendipity suggests the arrival of good fortune in an unsought manner, or by a sort of good luck. Schizophrenia has taught me a great deal regarding the serendipitous.

If I had had the ultimate choice of whether or not to live with schizophrenia, quite frankly, currently, I would have it no other way. Schizophrenia has delivered its fair share of rationed suffering, and this is true. Nevertheless, schizophrenia has been serendipitous too. In inadvertent ways, schizophrenia has led me to positive life qualities as well. For example, prior to this book, I wrote two other ones. Never would I have authored books without the arrival of schizophrenia. Unconditionally, schizophrenia has been my muse. Beyond any doubt, I certainly enjoy writing as an activity and this has been a most pleasing sort of by-product. Additionally, I have also given several talks about living with schizophrenia, including at in-person forums and also on the radio and certain podcasts. In regards to my books and my speaking, to be considered as a potential example for others is tremendously honorific and beyond humbling. As I previously mentioned, schizophrenia also changed my career path serendipitously, from broadcasting to the mental health field. If not for schizophrenia, not even a modicum of such an idea would have flashed across my mind—to pursue work in the field of social work. Further, without a doubt, the mental health field, despite my experiences with schizophrenia, is profoundly more aligned with my given aptitudes and intellectual interests than broadcasting was. These are all examples of serendipitous good fortune from my schizophrenia. I mention serendipity because, if ever so lucky, you may too, at one time or another, make its acquaintance. In terms of vocational creativity, when serendipity gestures in your direction please take note of it and consider what it offers. It may just be a most positive and unexpected life opportunity. In a greater sense, serendipity very capably presents amid the fictional lines drawn by the vocational zigzag.

Schizophrenia taught me career life lessons. Vocational pursuits need not have any requisite to proceed according to a normative or expected trajectory (that is, if normative, if according to the general construct, it necessarily applies in all cases). Personally, schizophrenia taught me the art of the "vocational zig-zag" and I admire its inherent aesthetic. Who cares if you must zig-zag? It should trouble no one. Simply do your best in your vocation, and dignity and pride will certainly follow.

Chapter 13

Cognitive Temperance

Lesson—Reasonableness is paramount.

Schizophrenia, according to its offer, induces psychosis. By its nature, psychosis entails a degree of erraticism, or the personal display of a highly irrational persona or disposition. More succinctly, psychosis coalesces in the form of consistent and vigorous irrationality. A presenting psychosis can be inferred by observers as secondary to routine conduct, across time and contexts, marked by an obvious form of irrationality. Such irrationalities can manifest in many ways and these types are clinically classified. Regarding irrational behavior, the applied illustrative clinical terms may include disorganized thinking, tangential or circumstantial speech, self-dialoguing, expressions of word salad, exemplars of bizarre beliefs, and stereotyped behavior. More specifically, for example, tangential speech entails an individual frequently leaving a topic of conversation with a focus on irrelevancy relative to the conversational topic.

Self-dialoguing is when an individual persistently talks aloud to oneself, including often the characteristic of a certain sort of self-mumble. If someone claims to be a "zillionaire", and I take this example from my own clinical work, such an expression is both fallacious and characteristically bizarre. Stereotyped behaviors are behaviors that are repeated; for example, a persistent self-rocking that serves no functional capacity. Psychosis and regular irrationality are tightly conjoined, and there are many ways that an individual may display them. The more psychotic or irrational the behavior may be, the easier, of course, it can be deciphered. If such observations are found and clinically verified, the phenomenon entails an individual breached from reality and it follows that they are someone who is observed as and consequently irrational.

Schizophrenia has taught me the life lesson of the value of pure reason. Make no mistake, I continue to experience psychotic-like thoughts, but I have developed insight along with the paramount skill of practicing rationality. I used to have psychotic cognitions with associated and consequent psychotic behaviors. During the first onset of psychosis, my speech and behavior were highly irrational and this eventually led to my diagnosis. I was an interpersonal and social mess. My verbiage was regularly out of proper context, bizarre, and highly inappropriate. My behavior, too, was also bizarre and often inappropriate. For example, on the occasion of a family picnic, I repeatedly made inappropriate statements. According to my psychosis, I was entirely cognitively and internally preoccupied and consequently my recurring verbalizations were nowhere near close to those of proper social contact. Over the course of that day, I made repeated bizarre and non-sensible utterances. Ultimately, I was so out of social context that my behavior at that family gathering was the impetus for a family intervention to get me some medical attention, which ultimately proved to be psychiatric care. Another example, when I was on the job decorating cakes, I again was so internally preoccupied according to my psychotic thoughts that I would often work an eight-hour shift and not say eight words total. Others would comment that I never spoke. This quietness was because I was amid psychotic thoughts, including the delusional belief of mind-to-mind communication. Indeed, I thought I was highly communicative, but only through the conduit of direct mind-to-mind communications, that is to say, without the need for spoken words. When others commented on my quietness, I was substantially dumbfounded because I thought I was significantly communicative. Such a lack of spoken word is clinically referred to as a poverty of speech, and this was certainly at the time well-qualified. This sort of quietness, induced by psychosis, spanned for weeks or longer. While amid psychosis, and prior to my developing insight, over the span of months (and approaching a year), I repeatedly made inappropriate conversation. Such levels of appropriateness were, according to clinical classifications, illustrative of inappropriate and tangential speech, combined delusions, bizarre behavior, disorganized thinking, attributable auditory hallucinations, and a generalized and prevailing psychosis. During this span of time, both my behavior and speech were erratic and, over time, increasingly so. I frequently spoke out without any sort of proper social context and my behavior followed. All this persistent inappropriateness was due to my cognitive psychosis. In this way, I was breached from reality.

At that time, I had no personal insight. I did not know I had schizophrenia. My conglomerate of irrationalities was florid and the display was an atrocious form of interpersonal conduct. After I was diagnosed, educated, and better acclimated to my schizophrenia, I incrementally began to put all the pieces together and I gathered a new awareness.

Firstly, I learned to recognize my irrationalities, profound they may be. I learned to identify my cognitive irrationalities and how they can drive associated inappropriate social behavior. I have come to a full appreciation of my cognitive distortions, which are predictive of my cognitive psychosis. Once I began to recognize my cognitive misgivings, then followed the impetus for a very primary form of personal coping. So, paramount to this, was this new gleaned coping skill and ability to recognize; I dare say it, it was a game-changer for my world.

Schizophrenia is a primary "thought disorder". Learning to overcome this primary cognitive mental illness, I first had to identify my cognitive distortions. It took me some time, many years, with continuing refinements to this very day, for me to recognize and identify my underlying distortions and irrationalities. I now can take holistic and comprehensive stock of my cognitive status, both when symptomatic and when at my healthy and best baseline. For example, I now know when I am traveling amid psychotic terrain. In general, perceptions are derivative of one's conglomerated sensory input, and, in my case, I have acquired the necessary skill of being able to identify my perceptions that are askew, distorted, and psychotic. From my mind's eye, in a manner of speaking, I now know what psychosis looks like. Due to my innumerable psychotic experiences, I now know when my senses are triggering erroneous perceptions. When amid a prevailing psychosis, I can now relax and I no longer panic; I no longer feel the need to run for the exit. Because it is now so familiar, like the back of my hand, I can recognize my cognitive psychosis. Such recognition was half the remedy. It's corollary, therefore, followed by the sequela of recognizing my psychosis, was then followed by corrective intervention. Such an intervention is characterized by needed self-talk, in conjunction with my acquired skill of managing my behavior; that is, not behaving in a way beyond the proper social context expects, or otherwise behaving erratically. Certainly, at one time, I did indeed behave erratically, but this now has been corrected so as to be extinct.

I have learned to practice what I call "rational social behavior". I learned this skill, despite a prevailing psychosis, to manage my behavior within a general social context. I have made it my mission to monitor my conduct, or behavior, when in a social milieu. In other words, I willfully implore myself to follow a steadfast rational conduct when in an interpersonal context. Now, my behavior will not stray from normative social conduct. I will not speak or behave beyond a proper social context. I fervently urge myself to remain most reasonable in a social context. I say nothing that may come out of left field. I behave with due decorum.

Conversely to identifying my psychosis, I now also know when I am amid non-psychotic thought. When such is the case, my thoughts are accompanied by no distress and I find myself in a restful sort of emotional ease. Additionally, when experiencing normative thought characteristics, my perceptions lack the sort of intensity present while wrestling with a psychosis. As such, my thoughts and perceptions will be like the waves of an ocean washing on the shore, that is, a calming sort of repetition. When I am amid healthy thoughts, the tsunami of schizophrenia reduces comfortably and settles into my psychological recesses. At such times or moments, I can settle into a preferable sort of cognitive equanimity.

The rest of this story is about an amazing dynamic. To this day, I continue to experience a sort of psychosis. It is, however, a purely cognitive sort of psychosis. I can recognize the psychosis in my thoughts. But the absolute game changer was my acquisition of the skill of not acting out as a consequence of my cognitive psychosis. So, the rub is that I may have thought a psychotic characteristic, but no longer does it disable. Ever steadfastly and diligently, will I act against these thoughts leading to manners of erratic social behavior. In terms of my behavior, I stay ever true to the interpersonal context, but psychotic thoughts prevail nevertheless. I have learned to live with cognitive psychosis, but absent of an associated psychotic type of behavior. In this sense, due to my effective functioning in the interpersonal realm, I avoid the ever-important term of functional disability. Regarding said term, for someone to qualify as having an active psychosis, one's ability to normatively function must be impaired over time and contexts. Normative functioning entails capability and effectiveness regarding one's generalized daily living activities, i.e., activities related to work, chore responsibilities, reasonable social activity, money management, med management (if applicable), and good hygiene as a few examples. If one's daily living activities are competent across time and contexts, the functional qualifies as capably inherent and effective and the psychosis is then clinically considered in retreat, latent, or perhaps even absent. Accordingly, my current schizophrenia diagnostic has been mitigated and I am largely considered recovered. Because I function well, such a characteristic decapitates an active schizophrenia qualifier, that is, involving one's level of diminished functioning.

Regarding my life experiences with schizophrenia, I find an ultimate and fascinating associated irony. Schizophrenia is a primary cognitive disorder that produces distortions, irrationalities, and erratic speech and behavior. As a generalized subjectivity, schizophrenia reigns as a primary inducement for such highly irrational conduct. Schizophrenia, characteristically, entails a florid irrationality. I find it most ironic that a mental disorder with the primary characteristic of irrational inducement taught me the value of tempered reason. Schizophrenia is entirely an irrational subjectivity. However, from it I have learned the value of pure reason.

A sense of reason, for us all, can help. As I have noted, we all fall prey to cognitive distortions, schizophrenia or otherwise. When one recognizes hyperbole in one's conduct, or in speech, cognitive distortion will reside there. Recognizing one's own irrational hyperbole can often times assuage and empower someone to be a better self. The power of reason can diminish maladaptive behavioral outliers and can significantly calm the waters of one's life. Further, schizophrenia has also has taught me numerous life lessons and has consequently provoked a much greater and deeper appreciation for life, including the sentiment to go forth and teach these lessons, so that others may benefit from them.

About the author

Robert Francis was diagnosed with schizophrenia in 1995. He earned a bachelor's degree in 1993 and a master's degree in social work in 2006. Robert has been practicing as a talk therapist for more than a decade. He is currently a licensed clinical social worker (LCSW). Regarding the topic of schizophrenia, Robert has authored two other books. His first book is titled *On Conquering Schizophrenia: From the Desk of a Therapist and Survivor* and his second book is titled *The Essential Schizophrenia Companion; With Foreword by Elyn R Saks, PhD, JD*. Each book, including this newest one, combines clinical and lived experience perspectives. Such a dual perspective of schizophrenia is both most novel and very illuminating. Robert's passion is to help others with schizophrenia to recover, as he did, and to live full, satisfying, and hopeful lives. Robert sees schizophrenia as having associated inherent strengths, and in *Schizophrenia: A Strengths Perspective; Life Lessons Learned from Living with Schizophrenia*, he brings these exemplary strengths to light for others to see, share, and appreciate. In *Schizophrenia: A Strengths Perspective; Life Lessons Learned from Living with Schizophrenia*, Robert accentuates the positive, and, as is customary of his writing style, he does so with characteristic warmth and an undeniable and touching appeal.